THE FLATNESS AND OTHER LANDSCAPES

The FLATNESS

AND OTHER LANDSCAPES

Essays by Michael Martone

THE UNIVERSITY OF GEORGIA PRESS   ATHENS AND LONDON

Published by the University of Georgia Press
Athens, Georgia 30602

Designed by Sandra Strother Hudson
Set in Monotype Walbaum
Printed and bound by Maple-Vail
The paper in this book meets the guidelines for permanence and durability of the Committee on Production Guidelines for Book Longevity of the Council on Library Resources.

Printed in the United States of America
00 01 02 03 04 C 5 4 3 2 1

Library of Congress Cataloging-in-Publication Data
Martone, Michael.
The flatness and other landscapes : essays / by Michael Martone.
p. cm.
ISBN 0-8203-2160-5 (alk. paper)
1. Martone, Michael—Homes and haunts—Middle West.
2. Authors, American—20th century Biography. 3. Authors, American—Middle West Biography. 4. Middle West—Intellectual life. 5. Middle West—In literature. I. Title.
PS3563.A7414Z469 2000
814'.54—DC21 99-16606

British Library Cataloging-in-Publication Data available

Winner of the Associated Writing Programs Award for Creative Nonfiction

For

SAM MARTONE and NICK PAPPAS

Latitude and Longitude

CONTENTS

ACKNOWLEDGMENTS

"The Flatness" appeared in the *Iowa Review.*

"Future Tense," "Pulling Things Back Down to Earth," "The Proper Levels of Vacuum," "Why the Windmill?" "Living Downtown," and "Correctionville, Iowa" appeared in *North American Review.*

"Stories We Tell Ourselves" appeared in *High Plains Literary Review* and *Narration as Knowledge: Tales of the Teaching Life,* edited by Joseph F. Trimmer and published by Heinemann.

"Iconography" appeared in *Falling Toward Grace: Images of Religion and Culture from the Heartland,* edited by J. Kent Calder and Susan Neville and published by Indiana University Press.

"The Other Houses in Eldon, Iowa" appeared in *Borderline.*

"Flyover" appeared in *Imagining Home: Writing from the Midwest,* edited by Mark Vinz and Thom Tammaro and published by the University of Minnesota Press.

"Manufacturing Place" appeared in *Northwest Review* and was reprinted in *Harper's.*

"Walking Beans" appeared in *Iowa: A Celebration of Land, People, and Purposes,* edited by Craig Canine and published by Meridith Publications.

"The Night Shift" appeared in *Flyway.*

. . . .

I thank Jane Brown Dupuis for inviting me to her family's farm near Turin, Iowa, and her family for receiving me so patiently and warmly. I thank Tom Williams, Rosalie Ahrendson, and Steve Gulick, who also allowed me to visit their families and farms. In Iowa, many people helped me get to know the place. I thank Joseph Geha, Mary Swander, Steve Pett, Susan Carlson, Marilyn Sandidge, and my colleagues in the English Department at Iowa State University. I gardened with Sam Pritchard. Clare Cardinal introduced me to the architecture of space and absence. I thank Jennie VerSteeg, Anne Hunsinger, Kim Kamizi, Robert Slocum, and all my students in Ames. I thank the editors and writers who supported these efforts, especially Robley Wilson Jr. of *North American Review,* David Hamilton of the *Iowa Review,* David Milofsky, Robert O. Greer, Mark Kramer, Wendell Berry, Richard Rhodes, Scott Russell Sanders, and Paul Zimmer and Holly Carver of Iowa University Press, who published *A Place of Sense* and *Townships.* I'd also like to thank Monroe Engle, Chris Leland and Osvaldo Sabino, Susan Dodd, Lucie Brock-Broido, Lewis Hyde, Verlyn Klinkenborg, Nancy Esposito, David Rivard and Michaela Sullivan, and my colleagues and students at Harvard. I thank Melanie Rae Thon, Margaret Himley, Susan Edmunds, John W. Crowley, Safiya Henderson-Holmes, Paul Maliszewski, and all my students at Syracuse. I thank my colleagues in Alabama (below the bug line), Sandy Huss, Robin Behn, Lex Williford, Bruce Smith, and Sara Davis. Susan Neville, Michael Rosen, and Michael Wilkerson and Deborah Galyan know this flatness. Thanks to Sallie Gouverneur and Doe Coover who landed the book. Thanks to Courtney Denney for visiting the Midwest. Thanks especially to Kathy Hall and Leighton Pierce. And thanks to Theresa Pappas who brought the Dodge Dart out to the middle border.

THE FLATNESS

They are thinking about Northern Ohio, about Indiana, about the long stretch through Illinois and on into Iowa. It is flat. The geometry of the fields suggests a map as large as the thing it represents. The squared township roads score the axes of coordinates. The cusp of trees on the horizon, the water tower, the elevator are tokens slid there representing ground taken and held. The only dimension marked by *z* is the state of dreaming as they drive on the interstates meandering in tangents that seek what the builders of railroads, who were here with rulers first, called a water-level route.

There are places in the Midwest that are not like this—the limestone hills, the loess bluffs, the forest lakes and sand dunes, the rills and knobs and kettles. But the people who know the place only by driving through it know the flatness. They skim along a grade of least resistance. The interstate defeats their best intentions. I see them starting out, big-hearted and romantic, from the density and the variety of the East to see just how big this country is. They are well read, and they see an expanse as they come out of the green hills and the vista opens up, a true vision now so vast that at night as they drive the vastness can be merely suggested by the farmyard lights that demonstrate plane geometry by their rearranging patterns. And, in the dawn around Sandusky, they have had enough, and they hunker down and drive, looking for the mountains that they know are out there somewhere. They cannot see what is all around them now. A kind of blindness afflicts them, a pathology of the path. The flatness.

It *is* flat. I grew up on a plain that was once the floor of a shallow inland sea scoured by four or five glaciers. On the interstate, when I drove from Fort Wayne to Indianapolis, the overpasses scaled above the country roads and railways. On either side of the ascending ramp little right-triangle lakes glistened. The holes, now topped with water, had provided the fill for the overpass ramps illustrating some law of conservation that you can only go as high as you go deep. From the artificial vantage of these overpasses, I could see, yes, for miles to the islands of trees or the yawing barn, a house on a reach. And way off in the distance, the land almost met the paralleling sky, the flat-bottomed clouds, and there, between the land and clouds, hung a strip of air without color that the sun set through.

It is flat for the people who drive through, but those who live here begin to sense a slight unevenness. As I drove down the perfectly straight highway, I waited for the gentle natural rise, no overpass, like a jet at the moment of take-off, before the climb, just as the front wheels of the plane leave the ground. And then I'd drop back down and cross a bridge over a river, the Wabash, the Salamonie, or the Mississinewa. The bump had been the end moraine of a glacier. The river is still in place from the melting and washout. These ridges are scalloped together on the plain like tidelines on a broad beach, a few extra grains of sand. I know it isn't much, a slight elevation that could be missed if you were fiddling with the radio dial. But to such a scale has my meter been calibrated. Living in a flat country, I began to read the flatness, to feel the slight disturbances in the field, to drive over it by the seat of my pants.

And on the plain where I grew up, there is a continental divide. Unlike the more famous one in the Rockies, in Indiana it is a matter of a few feet. Two rivers meet in the city of Fort Wayne and the third one they form flows back on the tributaries. It looks strange on a flat map, like a dual-lane highway. The new river heads back north and east paralleling its headwaters going the other way. Rain falling on the east side of Fort Wayne eventually finds its way to the Atlantic. On the west, the rainfall will travel to the Gulf of Mexico. It is a matter of a few feet.

Growing up there, I tried to imagine continental watersheds sloping away from me. I lived in a neighborhood called North Highlands. Before the developers came up with that name it was known as Hungry Hill because one winter horses couldn't haul food-laden drays up its icy slopes. It isn't much of a hill. But it is another ending of a glacier. It is just high enough so that it is the only part of town that never floods. Since I've been alive, Fort Wayne has had three hundred-year floods. The flooding is due to the flatness. After a heavy rain or a good snowmelt, water everywhere begins to rise, in the rivers, the ditches, the gutters. It pools in sheets on the saturated ground. It can't run off since the ground is level. Instead, it rises. There is a skim of water in the streets. The parks are lakes. The flooding is gradual. Often it takes days. The water is finding a balance, finding the contour that runs through the town like a fault, before it moves. The water keeps rising and spreading. The water, never running very fast in the riverbeds, stops altogether now, quivers at the brim of the old levees like that lip of water a couple of molecules thick that shimmers above the rim of a full glass. Fort

Wayne floods are slow disasters with people going to work as usual while others pump their basements or fill sandbags. There is always plenty of warning. There is always nothing to be done. There is not much raging water. Homes are inundated at the same speed it takes to repaint them. And when the owners repaint the houses, they dash a little line on the doorsill to mark the high water of the flood.

The flatness informs the writing of the Midwest. The flatness of the landscape can serve as a foil, the writing standing out, a kind of Blue Hotel, in opposition to the background. There is enough magical realism to go around here. A friend, Michael Wilkerson, goes so far as to call the Indiana Toll Road the Bermuda Triangle of Highway Travel. It's true. People who drive through the state have stories. They report mysterious breakdowns, extradimensional rest stops, the miraculous appearances of state troopers. In the whiteout of the passage through the flatness, dreaming can take over. The dull colors richen. The corn in the field begins to sparkle like the cellophane corn on the set of the *Wizard of Oz*. And that movie with its film noir depiction of the Midwest suggests another way of capturing this place.

I can still remember Danny Kaye introducing the movie on TV, telling the kids at home not to worry, that the black and white of Kansas was just the way they made the picture. Then as now, those grays of the monotonous landscape interested me more than the extravagant color. I have my mirages, but they are nothing fancy—the mirror of water that coats the hot road ahead reflects the flat sky and galvanizes the horizons. For me this Midwest is the perfect setting, this matter of a few degrees, a few feet either way. Here is ground that turns at once into swamp then into sea, each a solid calm surface. Beneath them all is a slight tilt, a tendency really, a bias so subtle you never notice you've crossed a line, that you've reached a crisis, that your whole world has changed.

I dislike the metaphor of the Heartland. True the Midwest is somewhere near the physical center of the map of America. But the Heartland implies that here, at some exact center, lies something secret, hidden and important, an X for a buried treasure. The Midwest is too big to be seen like that. I think of it more as a web of tissue, a membrane, a skin. And the way I feel about the Midwest is the way my skin feels and the way I feel my own skin. The Midwest as hide, an organ of sense and not power, delicate and coarse at the same time. The Midwest transmits in fields and waves. It is a place of sense. It sometimes differentiates heat and cold, pain and pleasure, but most often it registers the constant bombardment, the monotonous feel of feeling. Living here on the great flat plain teaches you this soft touch. Sensation arrives in huge sheets, stretched tight, layer upon layer, another kind of flood.

Perhaps I make too much of geology, topography imprinting on our lives. It was the Romantics of the last century who gave us mountains as something beautiful to see instead of impediments to cross. From them too we have inherited "the view." I grew up in a landscape not often painted or photographed. The place is more like the materials of art itself—the stretched canvas and paper. The midwestern landscape is abstract, and our response to the geology of the region might be similar to our response to the contemporary walls of paint in the museums. We are forced to live in our eyes, in the outposts of our consciousness, the borders of our being. Forget the heart. In the flatness, everywhere is surface. This landscape can never take us emotionally in the way smoky crags or crawling oceans can. We stare back at it. Beneath our skins, we begin to disassemble the mechanisms of how we feel. We begin to feel.

FUTURE TENSE

Time is all mixed up here. "Here" is Riverside, Iowa, and the reason Time is all mixed up has to do with the way people here are forced to talk about the town's main attraction. Well, it isn't quite an attraction yet. There is a committee working on that. But what the attraction will be once they get it going is that Riverside, Iowa, is the future birthplace of James T. Kirk. James T. Kirk is a character from *Star Trek,* a television show about the future that was canceled years ago. This adds to the confusion. People have to talk about the television series in the past tense, fondly, nostalgically. It's over and done, existing in reruns. But the people of this small Johnson County town are planning events that will have happened (is that even a tense?) sometime in the next century.

By all accounts this was Steve Miller's idea. I spent a rainy spring day looking for Steve Miller to ask him about it—to get the history of this thing that will happen. As I looked for him I visited the sites of importance in the future boyhood life of a made-up boy who would become, in his own future, a starship captain. During that day in Riverside, Iowa, I transported back and forth through this warp in time, but also I traveled through the thin membrane of fact and fiction. I saw what had happened and what will happen and what people had wanted and wished to have happen, to have happened, to have had happen.

In the consignment store on First Street, I picked through an old cigar box full of yellowing decals and hand-lettered buttons that said things like "Riverside, Iowa: The Future Birthplace of Captain James T. Kirk." The woman who ran the store helped some older women exchange condensed novels for other condensed novels.

"I've read that one. And that one. And that."

"That was a good one."

On the decal was a silhouette of the town—a low bushy outline of the tops of trees with the water tower and the steeple of the Church of the Assumption pushing through. The message was "Trek your way to Riverside, Iowa," in a futuristic organic type. But that skyline was instantly recognizable as that of another town time forgot—sleepy and shaded, holy and watered. Riverside does have a pleasant seat rising in steps from the valley. The river is the English. The abandoned rail bed follows the river's trek. First Street, the highway, a step higher, runs parallel east and west. And above that the red-brick fronts of the buildings of town, the terraced lawns of the white houses above and beyond, and beyond that the massive Assumption and its lesser buildings—convent, rectory, academy, and school—on the very summit of this old round-shouldered hill. It must have been lovely. It must have been obvious when some unremembered town founders saw the place for the first time and founded. This is, this was the place, their place.

It isn't truly a town that time forgot. That implies that nothing changed, changes, of course. Later, I looked up at the town from a rail siding near the grain elevator in the valley. Sparrows were diving into some spilled and spoiling corn on the ground. The tracks were gone, the roadbed nearly invisible. The stores on First were all gone, the sidewalk still raised wagon-bed high above the road for the easy exchange of goods. There were a few bars. A branch bank. The consignment shop. Rainwater ran down the streets that led up to the church, the heavy clouds seemed a few inches above the steeple's point.

"It came to him in a bar, I think." The woman who ran the consignment shop was telling me about Steve Miller's idea. "Something had to be done. Look around," she said. She had grown up in Riverside, remembered the farmers coming to town and the Amish in their wagons. "The birthplace is right next door, or will be," she told me. "Last summer, during the first festival, they put up a little marker. I don't know if it made it through the winter. I haven't looked." She said she was still surprised they came—the busloads of strangely dressed people who watch the television show and go to things like this dressed like characters from their favorite episodes. Aliens walked the shattered sidewalks. They wore capes and mail and green makeup. They came from Chicago, a busload. A woman from Los Angeles flew in in her own plane. The campgrounds were guarded by kids carrying ray guns. They bought decals and stickers.

I could tell she was unsure of the idea. "Something has to be done," she said again.

"It works, doesn't it?" I said, "I mean, I came because of it, I guess." I was out of season though, she said, laughing a bit. Next week, March 26, would be the actual birthday.

. . . .

Somewhere in all those episodes of *Star Trek* there is a mention of Captain Kirk's birth. It took place in Iowa, of course. You fill in the attendant mythology of values that this shorthand would lend to a character, to the character's character—hardworking, honest, independent, loyal. All of it. Steve Miller wrote to the producers of the show and claimed to be Kirk's kin. Sure, why not? they said. Riverside it is. Plans were made then for this annual festival in the summer, part of the schedule of festivals celebrating the harvest of various species of local produce, the circuit of centennials, the founding of railways that no longer survived. All the special days—Norwegian, Swedish, Czech, Dutch. The signs on the outside of town were changed. They once read, *"Riverside—where the best begins."* Now *"Trek"* has been substituted for *"best,"* a line painted lightly through the latter so you can see both, hedging. The population is 826.

There is not one Kirk listed in the Riverside phone book. Most of the names look like German to me. Steve Miller is trying to find a family named Kirk to move to town, the angel Gabriel with an annunciation. That is what the secretary in the city attorney's office told me. "He's trying to get somebody here to change their name. Anything." The attorney is leaning in the doorway of the office professionally involved in the finer points of the statue saga. Steve Miller wants to have a statue built in the park of the young James T. Kirk leaving Riverside for the space academy. William Shatner, who played the character of James T. Kirk, won't give permission to use his likeness since his likeness was, at the time, a policeman on another television show. And the lawyer wonders about this—who owns the likeness of a made-up person, whether they need to ask permission of the actor at all. I can tell he has thought about this in his spare moments. To him and to his secretary all of it is so curious. They tell me to go look at the pile of rocks in the park. That is where the statue will be, of the young Kirk going off to space.

"Where do they go?" I asked about the young people of Riverside. They are going away, obviously, and their leaving is not commemorated. There is nothing here for them to do. It is literally a sleepy little town, most folks driving up to Iowa City to work, driving back here for bed. As we talk we keep running into the time problem. The town's only claim to fame is something that has yet to happen, that will never happen, that they want in a half-hearted way to make happen.

There are little statues of Mary housed in little grottoes in many front yards. A Catholic town. The blue of her robes is often bleached and bled to a robin's-egg blue. And on the breasts of some of the figures is a dollop of red, the heart that remembers so much, a spring flower pulsing in the shadows of the brown evergreens. The Church of the Assumption *is* something. It is on the Registry of Historic Places. The woman in the consignment shop said that people came from all over the countryside to build the church. It is red brick, huge yet functional, vernacular and honest. If it were even older than it is, even though it is registered as historic, maybe people would come to Riverside to look at it and leave a few dollars behind in this town. Mary, above the main door, is at least twice the size of life. She is being taken into heaven whole, her clothes billowing, suggesting a sucking whirlwind, a midwestern twister. Her clothes wrap back around her and cling to her upraised arms. Her clothes are becoming clouds. Her flesh too—clouds, air, pure white heaven.

I've been told that I can buy a vial of Kirk Dirt. It has been scooped from the birthplace. Steve Miller owns the lot that will one day be the birthplace. As I walked from the city attorney's to the lot that will one day be the birthplace, I did kind of get into the spirit of the thing. I imagined children playing in this alley, which still is a cinder alley. Of course my imaginary children were imagining within their games the people they would become, stopping now and then to rewrite, in elaborate collaboration, the history of their future and starting over again now more confident, more clear about where they were heading.

. . . .

Okay, I admit I've watched *Star Trek* in its endless reruns. I love the parts where Kirk, the boy from Iowa, rages when his crew has been shanghaied from him. His crew, like Odysseus's men, are always succumbing to the eating of the lotus, easily accepting the paternal and protective care of some alien superior race. And Kirk rages. It never works for him, this future of bliss. He tells us. He tells his crew. He tells the sad-eyed aliens too. Man, he says, must struggle. Human beings must always be improving, perfecting, restless and unsatisfiable. It takes a while for the crew to stop acting like kids, to grow up and act like adults. These grown men in funny outfits. And these children here pretending in my imagination, exactly duplicating the stories they have absorbed from TV. The scripts of television are their scripts. Life is already becoming, will always be becoming, lived somewhere else.

There were no children in the alleys playing. In the drizzle, I did not look for long for the stick that was supposed to mark the future birthplace. There was junk in all the backyards. Old rose trellises needed painting. Clotheslines sagged with the invisible weight of ghost laundry. Here and there on some rooftops and backyards were the satellite dishes all pointing up to space.

It is plain, isn't it? Obvious to you now that this town will not survive to the future, to the time, if there will be one, of the miraculous birth. The birth that the rebirth of the town is staked on. Riverside will be lucky to make it deep into this new century. You know it. The people who remain know it. And Steve Miller, wherever he is, maybe even he knows it too.

Up the road to the west is Kalona, Iowa, another small town. It is thriving. I stopped there for pie, and the cafe was closed, only for remodeling, to expand. The town has two Main Streets. One is for the cars. The other is for buggies and horses. The Amish materialize in the alleyways. Do their business. And disappear. Sure, people come to catch a look at them. The stores all have the Amish culture captured in charms and mementos of impulse purchases, souvenirs of the simple. But the tourist dollar, however large, cannot explain the health of the town. It is not the attraction of the Amish but the Amish themselves who drive the town. When they spend money they spend it here—the dry goods, the blacksmith, the hardware. It is an economy that sustains itself. It is a mistake to say it is living in the past.

Riverside, a few miles away, is nostalgic for its future. Its scheme for survival is a paradigm of many towns and cities where convention centers and shopping malls are only less-original lures for someone else's expendable income. These developments are models of recreation, not creation. Life is a species of entertainment in this model, not part of a community which sustains and enriches itself and which is a part of a larger community that does likewise.

Steve Miller, wherever he is, believes, as many of us do, that out there somewhere is a great new universe and that we should all go. Steve Miller is acting to save what is left of his dying town, I am convinced. What is sad is that his hope rests on a birth that never took place and, even in his wildest dreams, never will.

PULLING THINGS BACK DOWN TO EARTH

"There's one," Tom said. We were in the pickup truck driving through Hepburn, Iowa. On the outskirts of town was a little house. In the backyard, a satellite dish.

"That one's got a motor drive," Tom said. The truck was slowing down. There was a stack of wood propped against the south wall of the house. The plastic on the windows was ripped and flapping in the wind. The yard was mud. The dish was turned away from the house to the south. It didn't rock or sway in the wind, though the stalk it was attached to seemed puny. The dish was the color of used soap.

"They can aim the thing from inside the house." He smiled a little. "I'd say it's pulling in the Playboy channel right now." He could tell, he told me. There were really only two satellites up there. Low in the southern sky and a little lower. I asked him about scrambling the signal. He said that the cable companies keep threatening to do it.

We'd been out in the country around Villisca in Montgomery County in southwest Iowa. Tom was showing me the neighborhood. We'd been through Nodaway and Guss and Hawleyville, and now we were on the way back to his farm. It was the first thaw of the year, and the roads were sweaty and slick. And it did seem, as we wandered around, that the satellite dish was replacing the old metal, many-bladed, windmill water pump. Again it struck me how steady these dish antennae are, cocked ears, in the landscape that pitches and rolls even in the slightest breeze. The old windmills were constantly turning, creaking, the red fishtail bearing the blades into the wind. I suppose schoolchildren in the cities would still make the windmill the centerpiece of a farm portrait. Windmill, barn, silo. That's a farm. But in the country, farms are more likely to be made up of grain bins and sheds and long low confinement buildings that look something like mobile homes. And now these dishes: big plastic platters, pie pans, some made out of a metal netting with overlapping panels like a vegetable steamer, a black mesh strainer. Kitchen utensils grown big, gone feral.

I imagine that the windmills that look so natural on the farm today looked pretty silly when they were put up late last century, the newest item from the Sears and Roebuck catalogue. The way we change our thinking about industrial artifacts is curious. Iowa celebrates a covered-bridge festival every summer near Winterset. Wooden covered bridges, there is no doubt, have entered a realm of celebration, a time to marvel at the beauty and craft of these old things, to urge their preservation. I've noticed a change of wind in the feelings directed toward the iron and steel truss bridges that replaced the covered bridge. As concrete replaces the rusting hulks, the I beams, the rivets, the tie bars, the scrollwork in upper reaches of the iron, the rust itself take on new meanings. Nostalgia. Awe. Delight. There will be a metal-bridge festival soon.

The old windmill towers and the new dishes stand out like

the superstructure of ships at sea, identifying silhouettes. Sometimes the dish was rigged right into the ruins of the old well. The yard lights were coming on. We headed back to Tom's house to change for dinner.

. . . .

When you drive in the country you have to see the odometer. The odometer becomes something more than a rough measure of engine life considered in the used car lot. The roads on the map to Tom's house and farm were marked off in quarter miles, half miles. And landmarks. The white house, the bridge, the railroad track. The directions were like the old guidebooks, before signs.

I had rented a white car and I was taking much pleasure plowing along those roads, picturing the spray of mud along the sides. The roads were straight. I watched the numbers slip around on the odometer. A seven would roll up and outside there would be a turn, another straight road going up and down over the next hill.

This part of Iowa has hills. That's a big surprise to people, hills in Iowa. Every summer the *Des Moines Register* sponsors a bike race across the state that attracts many out-of-state participants. The newspaper files reports daily as the bikes head east. There is only one story to report, and the newspaper reports it over and over: the out-of-state riders are amazed at how hilly Iowa is. Below Interstate 80 are the foothills, then further south, the Alps of Iowa.

Because there are hills, more farms have more animals, the land in pasture grass and alfalfa instead of row crops. I saw plenty of cattle and hogs and sheep on both sides of the road. And the empty fields were fenced, which indicated animals were sheltering since the sky was close and snow would come and go.

Of course, I found the house. Tom probably had been giving those directions for years. I remember a class in junior high school called language arts that consisted, it seemed, of giving directions to get places in a city where I myself had never been.

I pulled into the driveway between the house where Tom had been born and the one where he grew up and now lived. I scrambled out of the car without my jacket. Really, I wanted to see the pattern of mud the front-wheel drive had created. It was cold in the wind. Tom came out of the feed mill and over the scale, up to where I was parked. I started in about how great his directions were, and how great what I'd seen of the farm was so far, how great it was for him to have me visit.

He was wearing blue-striped coveralls and a winter COOP hat with the flaps down. Resting on the bill was a white cloth mask he used when he worked in the confinement buildings. He looked younger than he did when he'd been my student because he'd shaved off his mustache. "It freezes outside in the winter and melts when I go in the buildings."

Tom had just started farming on his own, a partner with his father. He had graduated a couple of months earlier, in December, from Iowa State. Tom's brief time at home, his short time being a farmer, had nearly coincided with that year's farm crisis. There had been inklings of problems—bank closings, foreclosures, protests at farm auctions—before and after the election in November. But when he graduated, these regional news stories had begun to attract the attention of the nation. My visit was the weekend before the farm rally in Ames.

The national events that would later transpire that winter and spring had that classic narrative structure as it was shaped and presented by the storytellers of newspapers, radio, and television. I think it began with other stories, the "farm" movies that prefigured the rising action: white crosses in the town squares, the formation of a farm coalition, the Farm Bureau's convention in Hawaii. The climax of the Big Rally. The swift reversal: the veto. The falling action: the tattoo of President Reagan's remarks that week, a joke or a wince, that he should have kept the grain and exported the farmers, that he shouldn't have said anything since it didn't get a laugh. There is a closure there. It signals enough already. There are other stories to tell. And I think we've grown used to things being told this way, the world itself adhering to the unities of some ancient aesthetics or modern attention spans.

Tom was farrowing these twelve sows—those twelve sows were due to farrow this weekend. I wanted to see that. And I wanted to see how the drama was affecting him. Maybe try and detect if he realized or even noticed he had been cast in this larger story, a character in somebody else's play.

I met his father, Don. He was dressed like his son. He took off his glove to shake my hand. Tom said, "This is Don." Don looked me up and down. I had worn what I consider my work clothes. I was ready to go. Don said, "Well, you better get him something to wear."

. . . .

They wanted to feed the cattle before the ground got any softer that day or in case it rained or snowed and melted, which would make everything worse. The tractor would tear up the pasture as we'd go through it pitching bales from the hay wagon. Tom told me that his dad would be happy this summer because they'd be making improvements, building terraces in the fields. "You get to build some terraces, don't you, Don?" As we headed to the pasture to feed the cattle, Tom began the task of sorting out the land for me. His neighbors', his uncle's, his folks', his own. Their own land, terraces and pastures and animals. The terraces give the look of play to the landscape, the childish glee of the sandbox. Serious business though, long-term and short-term costs. It was remarkably clear to Tom and his dad. Build terraces. Don't break open the ground.

I had to climb a ladder. I realized the only time I climb ladders is when I visit farms. Always I am amazed to find out that my body is as heavy as it is when I have to haul it up. I expect there will be something to support my back, something to lean against, because this isn't an inclined stepladder tricking my center of gravity along the steep slant, but a straight shot up. Halfway up the side of a bin I always remember I don't climb ladders, don't really know how to. This ladder was wired to the outside of a pole shed where they kept the hay. I believe it was a ladder salvaged from a windmill, a mere wisp of a ladder.

I was in boots I'd never worn before. I had deerskin gloves that didn't move. Tom, of course, scrambled up ahead of me. The wind was blowing. The birds Tom had startled from the loft above blew away, their wings of no use.

Now we all put ourselves in these positions. I was here, a volunteer, jaunty, a good student, wishing to perform, to please. But I was already, at the foot of the ladder, in way over my head. I'm only a generation away from all this, as are many of you out there. I know lots of things, but not too many of them have to do with physical laws. It is like learning to crawl but without the instincts or genetic triggers a baby's got. Climbing a ladder. And I understood that to climb a ladder is why I visit farms in the first place. It's the old nagging doubt of the office worker. It's *doing* things. I'm not a participatory journalist. I don't want to farm and tell. The *Paper Farmer*. My curiosity brought me to the base of this flimsy ladder wobbling up the side of a swaying shed. When I moved to Iowa six years ago I would have drawn a farm with a silo, a barn, and a spinning windmill in the sun. I'm just getting to know my way around, getting to feel at home. As

I made ready to climb that ladder on the farm near Villisca, Iowa, there were in other parts of the country many people talking about what was happening on the Farm. I reminded myself, as a kind of pep talk, that those people didn't know the first thing about what was going on. As I swung onto the ladder I also understood that important things would be decided anyway without that knowledge.

. . . .

We went to the new place to feed some more cattle. The farms I visit are made up of new places and home places. If you ask a man who farms 400 acres what size is the right size for a family farm, he'll say 400 acres. Ask a man who farms 1,200 acres and he is likely to say the same. Couldn't make it below 1,200. The problems of this spring have a lot to do with scale—farming too much or not enough, growing or shrinking or disappearing. Don told me that this new place might have been a mistake. What he says is all understated. I'll never know the details. They bought when the land was much more expensive than it is now, now that it is falling rapidly. Don adds quickly that he isn't worried, that one good thing about Tom being a part owner is that they won't have to pay him.

Before they got the land, the hills had been cropped out in corn and soybeans. They put it into pasture. Terraces soon. We walked square bales from a barn to a stand of trees and there kicked the hay loose, another operation that I handled clumsily. The steers snuck up on us as we went back and forth, the ground sucking at our feet. Don talked a little about family history, more because he thought I wanted to hear it, I think, thought I expected it of a farmer. I remember his family history being a series of accidents, guesses, and compromises, like all histories. And I remember thinking that he was trying to disguise the haphazard past that brought us here, make it sound like there was a plan. Someone had sat down and thought all of this out. I kept kicking at the bales, pulling the twine. The cattle were patient with me. In the barn, Don pointed out the joints in the beams. Pegs instead of nails. It is his barn and he is proud of it, but nobody any of us knew built it.

. . . .

Don and Cherryl live in a new house they designed. I liked it. It has one big room downstairs—kitchen, dining room, living room. A fireplace and woodstove are across the room from a big window that looks out back over the hills and terraces. You can see three valleys on a clear day, Cherryl tells me. I could see, off in the middle distance, the pole shed, the one with the ladder. I stayed the night in a daughter's bedroom. She's away in college. Tom has his own house now.

The front yard is fenced, and, if times were better, Cherryl says, they'd run sheep there. On the wall next to the big window hangs the same scene done on a loom in wool, dyed the way it must look in fall. The house was designed so there was a room for Cherryl's looms and yarns.

During lunch Cherryl asked Tom if I knew what I was getting into. Tom let me answer, ate, listened to the basketball game. Don told her what we had done, looked outside and was happy we'd beat the snow. They figured out where everyone was going to be in the afternoon, including me. They asked me, and I told them what brought me here. We adjourned.

In the basement there was another room with an outside entrance where we changed again back into work clothes. When we came in earlier we took turns using the bootjack. My shoes had come off in the boots. But we weren't going to work exactly. And when we came in before lunch we hadn't really left work the way we left our clothes in the special changing room. It feels funny, not being used to it, not going to work, not going home. I'm a tourist here.

Driving from the new house to Tom's house and the hog houses, we almost clipped a mailbox planted close to the road on a curve. I sat between Tom and Don, who was driving. They talked about the history of that mailbox. How many times it's been knocked over, the motives the neighbor might have for putting it back up in the same place after each time. How they always forget it is there.

We all waved at a car going by in the other direction. Don—two fingers off the wheel. Tom—flick of the hand from the dash. Me—more of a nod of the head, trying to pass. It is in the timing, actually. Make a move too soon and the other folks can't see your subtleness. Too late, and they've gone talking about you. The people in the other car waved back.

At Tom's house we stopped on the road. Tom got out to get the mail. There's a clump of four mailboxes all with the family name. The mail is a big deal. Checking it is an important moment. Towns are towns because of post offices. Mail can be a daily confirmation that you are where you're supposed to be. Tom stood sorting the envelopes. Suddenly, a horn went off in the buildings. It sounded like a submarine about to submerge, general quarters. Tom sprang into the cab. Don gunned into the drive, shouting instructions to Tom. "I'll let you off at the barn!" My God, I thought, something's happened in one of the hog houses—a fire, they can't breathe, pigs are being born. We bounced over the yard. Tom had the door open, leapt and ran to the barn. "Dive! Dive!" the buzzer said.

It was the phone. Cherryl had called to say that Iowa had lost again.

. . . .

Tom got me a mask from the little shed that houses the scale. They keep the masks there for when buyers come on the farm. The mask I got was like the ones Tom and his father had perched on the bills of their COOP caps. Mine was whiter. It felt like felt. It had subtle indentations pressed into it, a ribbing, that made it cup my nose and mouth. There was a metal strip at the top. I crimped it around my nose. I fiddled the mask into place. Every time I went into the hog houses for the rest of the visit, I had to get a new mask out of the shed. They were in a box, nestled inside one another. I never learned the trick of storing one out of the way, like a visor, on my cap, whipping it down and in place when it was needed. My masks looked like used tissue after a few minutes, crumpled, stove in. The metal clip whitened where I tried to bend it back in shape, snapped in two. I'd wrestle the thing off my head, wedge the rubber band from my ears, stuff it in my pocket.

After all that, the mask didn't do any good. I had brought some allergy pills, antihistamines. I knew what I was getting into.

The hog houses are closed up tight in the winter. I was surprised by the flies. You forget flies over the winter, get to know them again slowly in the spring. They don't go away in the confinement hog house, where it is always like it is—warm, close, moist. The manure from the animals goes through slats in the floor, into holding tanks right below us. In late winter the pits were nearly full, four foot deep. It wasn't that it smelled bad. It just smelled. Sensitive sense. I wasn't used to using it. But the mask has nothing to do with smell. It's beyond smell. I was breathing, breathing in the pit gases, and my lungs were closing up shop.

Tom was showing me a table full of medicines, drugs. He had told me before how the use of the stuff concerned him, especially subtherapeutical, not for curing a disease in the animal, but to stimulate its growth. We were in a house that had thirty crates, a sow and a litter of a dozen, more or less, in each. I was trying to breathe and listen and see. A sow would stand up in her cage. Her pigs crashed around the pen getting out of the way. The tubular cage keeps the sow from rolling on the pigs when she lies down. It leaves room for the pigs to maneuver. I could hear water running, the snuffling at the automatic fountains, the squealing, the jostling. The pigs nearest me were curious, sniffing. It seemed Tom might be talking to himself, thinking out loud about the drugs. These were his animals, his building, his drugs. He had, however, bought into this system. He'd have done things differently, tried to think things through. But he could get no distance, no elbow room. There were pressures, forces that were beyond his control—bankers and markets and this system. These systems were new, still evolving. They had no track record. These things—the buildings, the economy, the method of production—had lives of their own. And in the building this other life, the pigs, still after all the study, finally, unknown and unknowable. They were looking at us. Tom poked at one of the big used syringes. The mask made it even more difficult for me to breathe. I felt that panic—suffocation, drowning, choking. It was in the air. Tom was in it every day. "You get used to it," he said. "But you do hear about what they're calling farmer's lung. Just like the miners get." My own drugs weren't doing a thing.

. . . .

In the farrowing house Tom was rearranging the crates, preparing the ones where the sow was about to give birth. He slid mesh flooring in over the slats so the newborn pigs wouldn't slip through. He gathered heat lamps, hung them on either side of the laboring sow.

The sows were due anytime. Tom had written to me saying, "Come on out." Attached to the letter was a list of dates and numbers of sows. The letter was done on his computer, a dot matrix printer. Tom had majored in computers and math at

Iowa State. Farm operations and agriculture classes hadn't interested him. He liked telling me about a farm-operation class he took where the instructor insisted a certain mower-conditioner be pulled by a sixty-five-horsepower tractor.

"I had cut thousands of acres with that very implement back home," he said, "and we never used more than thirty-five horsepower. I told the guy that. He didn't believe me. I went back home one weekend and looked in the manual. It suggested twenty-five."

In the arguments during those weeks of the farm crisis, the position that farming was a business like any other business came up often. It seems that the decision to return to farming or to leave it and work somewhere else does not come easily to farm kids. It is not like the usual vocational choice, this job or that one. It might be true that farming is like other businesses. But it *is* true that there are few businesses anymore that involve children the way farming still does. A land of opportunity implies a model of the world that is out there off your folks' land. Farm kids are different from city and suburban kids because they have this decision to make: stay or go. To the rest, to go is a given.

Tom came back to the farm. That means he will work with and be near his mother and father every day for a very long time. It is a state of affairs that is, by definition, insulated, and it is, by its rarity, a state further removed from that of the rest of America.

Tom's a quiet man. He does things. He does not talk about what motivated him, perhaps because he believes I could not begin to understand the reasons that brought him home to Villisca, or because he doesn't believe in words themselves, their processing, that matrix of dots.

One sow had been laboring too long, Tom thought. He slid on a clear plastic glove that covered his whole arm. He squirted on a disinfectant and reached up inside the sow. He said, "Everything seems all right. I don't get it." The sow was grunting and panting. Tom pulled his arm back out. He clutched a pig. It was alive. We watched for a bit, seeing if any more would follow. The newborn stumbled around on the mesh flooring. Tom put him under the heat lamp. We went on about the other chores. Every time we came back into the farrowing house, Tom checked the sow. He didn't want to induce contractions, the drugs again, but decided finally to go ahead. Tom had told me about the vet who wanted to abort the unborn piglets of newly bred gilts, pigs pregnant with their first litters. Doing so, the vet then could control the pigs' cycles, and gilts would give birth at the same time. This would take some more of the guesswork out of it.

I was able to breathe easier in the farrowing house. I don't know why. Tom went back to the nursery. I watched the sow and the one pig.

. . . .

I wandered around the yard. It was snowing again, big and heavy globs of snow. It wasn't sticking. My mask hung around my neck. It had somehow gotten turned inside out. I met Don coming out of the feed mill. He had been grinding feed. "The smartest thing my dad did," he said about the mill. He showed me the boars in their pens. He called a huge spotted one a wimp, said he was much happier with the Durocs. The sow I'd been watching was one of the group that had been artificially inseminated. He showed me an old hog house that he thought might start up again after a little work. I saw the honey wagon, the manure tank. Don wished the ground would freeze so he could pump the pits and spread it on the fields. He would have to do something with it. He didn't want to think about pumping it over the hill.

I asked him if he was coming up to the rally in Ames. He said he didn't think he had the time. He went on. His feelings about the whole thing were mixed. He thought some might have deserved it, borrowed too much. But there was bad luck, the breaks. He told about a neighbor who might be helping his neighbors *too* much, dropping things on his own place to go help. Tom and he had tried to translate what they did on the farm into the terms of a regular job, so many hours a week. They were working enough. Who wasn't? You compete with your neighbors as well as the folks in Canada.

I thought then of the telling phrase from the Vietnam War, of destroying the village to save it. What were those farmers going to fight for up in Ames? It seemed that what was being said about farms wasn't meshing. Was the farm the innovative frontier of agricultural science and enterprise? Or was it the repository of traditional beliefs and values? It also seemed that no one could approach farming without nostalgia both for the past and the future. It was this tug of war between longings. But what seemed to be longed for most was that the problems should be settled, fixed, taken care of, finished. No more manure in the pits. Or flies. Or problems in the farrowing pens. No more arguing in the commodity pits or congresses. Wanting it to be over and done with—that was the one clear message of the farm rally. By calling it a crisis, by treating these problems as if they were like a bad midwestern snow storm, we were able to ignore the fundamental issues as well as the daily realities that finally have no answers or solutions, like life or death. Some things simply must be done, not finished.

. . . .

Outside the nursery door was a dead pig. Its mother had crushed it. It was smashed on one side, waffled flat by the slats on the floor. It should have been big enough, smart enough, fast enough to get out of the way. There is a steady loss of pigs. It is hard to tell if the crates and pens constructed with this type of thing in mind might also contribute to it. In the alleys and gutters of both houses were dead pigs. Some were born dead. Some were runts that couldn't compete with the rest of the litter. There were not that many. But it didn't take many to notice.

Cherryl has told me how much Tom hates to kill the ones that have been crushed but aren't dead yet. Don has been taking care of that for a long time. Tom does it, but he can't get used to it.

I think about the Midwest sometimes as being the great graveyard for the country. People leave the Midwest to go live somewhere else. But bodies are always being shipped back to be buried here. I wonder if the rest of the country doesn't think of the Midwest as they would think of their local cemetery. Both are even landscaped the same—not too hilly, few sturdy trees, plastic flowers. People who don't live here are kind of proud that they can't be bothered with sorting out the I states—Iowa, Illinois, Indiana. They lose track of the family plots in the same way. Out of sight, out of mind. Only two seasons here. Winter and summer. Even to call the Midwest the heart of the country is not to get it right. It is more the gut. It is the gut of the nation. So why should we expect anyone to come visit? They fly over. They pass through (even better). The Midwest busied itself with changing the living into the dead, the dead into the living.

It's just messy here. Confinement houses, slaughter houses. Our houses. If the whole country were zoned by one big planning board, we all know what would be allowed to go on here. It goes on here anyway. Dirt. Dirt is us.

. . . .

I was outside the nursery door trying to catch my breath. It was raining now. I was balancing on a board that bridged a pool of muddy water. They had to regrade this part of the yard. The crushed pig was by the door.

Inside Tom was putting a litter of pigs into an old milk crate suspended from a scale. I had tried to gather up the pigs as they scampered around the pen, but I got winded instantly. I went back into the house. Tom was working smoothly, quickly. He was taking the gilts out of the milk crate, putting them back with their mother. I was trying to help Tom as he castrated the boars. I held their hind legs up, the pig head rested against my belly. Tom felt between their legs, pushed up, made two quick cuts with a scalpel. He squeezed out the testicles and cut the connecting cords. He swabbed on some disinfectant. I took the barrow back to the litter. Tom reached for the next pig.

I could do one litter at a time before I had to get outside in the cold air. Outside the nursery door was the dead pig. Water ran in sheets off the metal roof of the building. A board floated on the pool of mud until I stepped on it. The mill was grinding and mixing feed. I could hear the clanking of the lids on the feed bunks down in the finishing barns. Now it was snowing.

. . . .

Tom lives in the house he grew up in. The house where he was born is across the driveway. When he moved back home, he moved into that house. But it was too cold, too old, too big. He moved over to the newer house.

We changed out of our work clothes in the basement. The basement was filled with work clothes, boots, gloves, hats. Tom had told me he never had to buy a coat since all the companies gave coats to him.

It is a big old farmhouse, the type of house a city kid might draw when drawing a farmhouse. But there is nothing in it except a couch and a TV in the living room, a bed in the bedroom, a computer in the dining room. He has two cats. They were waiting for us at the head of the stairs.

He showed me his records, entered the litter weights he'd just recorded. Don hadn't kept detailed records. School paid off here. We were waiting to go up to his parents' house for dinner. We talked about basketball a little. Bobby Knight had just thrown a chair at a referee. Tom told me he wanted to get one of those satellite dishes so he could watch basketball. At college he played pickup games with the team, ran around with the players. Cherryl describes her son with the help of basketball.

"Tom," she said, "is always one-on-one."

We were exhausted. We drifted around the house. We played a game on the computer that had to do with outer space. Tom said it was the only game he had. The program recorded all of his scores from all the games he'd played. He purposely lost so we could watch the starship explode.

I looked at a catalogue from the semen company.

Tom waved his tax form at me. "Won't have to pay anything this year."

We sat on the couch. The cats roamed over us. I was thankful for the break.

Later, I drove us to the new house in my muddy rented car. After dinner, after his parents had talked with me, Tom's father drove him home. Together they checked the sows, walked the yard.

. . . .

Tom got the day off Sunday. He only gets every other Sunday off. He'll sometimes save up the days and take the whole weekend off. He wants to go to the Big Eight basketball finals in Kansas City. Tom had said that he didn't want to work for the big computer companies, didn't want to work for anybody. Of course, he is working for himself, and he does boss himself around. Still, in complex ways, he is an employee of the large companies that sell him equipment, chemicals, seeds, and the sperm that he depends upon, that give him bright jackets and caps, his uniform. He is aware of this. There is irony on the farm. It mixes with those sincere, rarely stated beliefs in hard work, family, and independence. But finally it isn't true independence at all. The debate that is going on in agriculture, beyond the immediate problems of debt restructuring, seems to be about what ways farmers will lose their independence. Will they become parts of corporate structures or of the ones that emanate from nature? Does happiness derive from subordination to instead of domination over the world? Which family are they to be part of? Which kind of work?

Since Tom had the day off, Cherryl and I were in the farrowing house doing teeth and tails and inoculations. Don had come home the night before saying that the sow Tom was worried about had had her litter. The twelve pigs were nosing into the teats, constantly rearranging their order, swarming. A sow in another crate was standing up, scraping the floor. She was lactating, the colostrum in pools beneath her. She would be next.

. . . .

Cherryl was dressed in brown coveralls, boots, and a hat. She didn't like to use the masks. She was standing in the alley between the crates trying to read the labels on the bottles. We were going to give the six-hour-old pigs injections to prevent scouring, a virulent form of diarrhea. There might have been an iron shot, too. We took the bottles and the needles and syringes over to the crate. I put a board across the top of the pen and we set up store. Cherryl reached in, grabbed a pig, and cradled it behind the front legs. She gave a shot into the right shoulder, put down the syringe, picked up the other one, and shot the left shoulder. She put down the syringe and picked up a livestock marker, a big crayon, and striped the pig's back. The stripe was bright pink, flamingo pink. The pink turned a kind of tangerine color under the heat lamp when she set him down. Him. That had to be done too today. Cherryl had to notch the ear to identify the pig as male or female. The day before, when we were castrating, Tom could read the ears on the pigs as we pulled them out. We found one notched wrong. "Cherryl must've done this group," he said. He asked me to remind him to tease her. He forgot. I forgot to remind him. As Cherryl readied for another pig I told her about the day before. She laughed.

I had just been watching her work, juggle all those operations. She asked me if I wanted to inject while she grabbed and marked.

I thought the pig was more nervous about being held than being shot. It settled down, stopped squirming in my hand after a moment. It thrummed, a little engine. No, that's not fair. It was not like a machine. But there was this tension and power. The belly was tight, harmonies under the skin. The cord was turning brown and trailed down along my arm.

When we were talking about sheep, and later, when he urged me to come back out for the calving, Tom had said that all baby animals are cute. Even this pig was cute. I gave him his shots. I was too gentle with the needle at first. I felt like I was trying to open a new jar of olives while I was in new clothes. Such fine tuning of strength. I tried to keep my eye steady on the correct dosage mark as the plunger went down. One big mark for one. Two half marks for the other. We finished the litter that way. It had gotten easier. The pigs were back in business, the pink stripes punching in and out. I couldn't breathe again. With my last breath I was making excuses to Cherryl, apologizing for having to leave her and get outside.

I waited outside the building. Snow now. Cherryl brought out a pig so I could see how the teeth and tails were clipped, the ear notched. These pigs will be in pens, and crowded in with other pigs. They'll nip at each other, bite tails and ears. Cutting the teeth, docking the tails is one response. The other, of course, is to change the whole system. Yesterday, as we worked, Tom talked about animal rights and people who do not farm who are concerned with the rights of animals. It was another delicate balance. He explained to me, perhaps a bit defensively, why he was doing this or that. No anesthesia for castrating.

Wouldn't do it at all if boars brought a price. It's another drug. Lose fewer pigs to weather, more to accidents. Fewer people have to raise the food.

I wondered if he thought about these moral ambiguities, these practical considerations while he worked, as he most often does, alone. The consequences of his actions are oftentimes right at hand. That is not to say that what he does or feels he has to do to animals is right or wrong, just that he is conscious. He considers. As I tried to breathe outside the farrowing house, I also understood that the way we all eat contributes to the way Tom works and the way Tom lives. Tom is as humane with his animals as he can be. Can we be more humane than Tom? Saying he has a will, a choice is not enough, I think, at least not enough until we look to our own choices, our own will.

Cherryl pried open the pig's mouth and showed me the needle teeth. She worked the cutters in and snipped off the ends. She held the pig between her legs. It seems there is a point with any animal where it will stop struggling, trying to get free. It is a kind of a freeze. Just a moment. Then more wiggling, twisting. In that moment, between breaths, Cherryl snipped the teeth, the tails. "Most times," she said, "there's little blood." The ears are encoded with a series of v'ed nips. Sex, litter, number in the litter. She'll work around the big ears. Clock positions. The edge of the cut flushed red, a pencil line. There had been so little color that weekend.

Cherryl went back in the house to finish the pigs. I stood out in the yard, cold and tired and sick. I would leave for home after lunch. I was alone and unable, really, to make sense yet of the weekend. Up in an oak tree, an old tree house, wet and rotting. I couldn't see any ladder or rope, no way up.

Tom came out of his house in his work clothes. He had his hands in his pockets. I didn't think he was going to work—it was his day off—but he might have thought he was going to watch other people work. Sometimes that is the best entertainment.

That's when we went for a ride through the country. We saw things that did not look good, dirt pooled in the ditches, equipment out in the open rusting, a new Butler building abandoned in a field. In the middle of another field was a used-car lot that Tom had never seen before. Everything looked worse because of the weather, the time of the year. The main streets of the towns were in ruins, not old enough yet to be transformed into places to come see, nor ghost towns, because there were people here. We could tell by the new dish in the side yard. There were people here watching TV.

In the yard outside the coliseum at Ames the day of the big farm rally, semitrailers circled a stand of satellite dishes. All the networks were there sending these pictures out into space. It might have been a basketball game, a graduation. Looking at the bright trucks, the gleaming dishes, I guess I felt connected to something. I thought of the dish Tom wanted, wanting to pull the whole world back down to earth.

Why should his life be more pure than my own, why should he conform to my notion of the farm generated by butter and bread commercials I've seen on TV, or to my image of what is rural or even poor? Our ghost towns are on the air, our ghosts too. Pictures without context. I think you should visit some of the hidden places of the country, farms and factories. Schools and offices. Get authorization to be admitted, become the author of what you witness.

Tom writes to me. They are out in the field collecting new calves. He tells me of the largest calf. His mother, for some unknown reason, has rejected him. They have to put her in a squeeze pen so she'll sit still and nurse. He writes to say that calving will go on for several more weeks, that he has twelve new litters of pigs. He writes to say he is a tired young farmer. He writes to say I should come back down to the farm.

THE PROPER LEVELS OF VACUUM

The heart of a milking system is the vacuum supplier, which produces vacuum in the pipes and tubes connected with it. The vacuum supplier must be of sufficient capacity to produce and maintain the proper vacuum level at each teat when all of the milking units are on-line. There must also be sufficient vacuum to move milk rapidly into the pails or through the pipeline. Maintaining the proper level of vacuum is very important on any milking system.

Handbook of Milking, produced by the DeLaval Separator Company

While Steve is working in the milk house, putting together the pails and claws, I am in the barn scooping out corn and protein to the cows. Steve has written out the rations on a brown paper towel. It is resting on the heap of ground corn in the wheelbarrow in front of me. The protein mix is in a plastic bucket. The cows are levering themselves up to their feet as I rush around them dumping the feed before their noses. One scoop for Molly. One and a half for Betty and a small scoop of protein. Amy gets two. The paper towel I'm reading from is like the ones Steve uses to massage the udders so that the cows will let down their milk. The radio is playing. A jazz show comes on at midnight. But I can hear the huffing the herd is making, tongues licking the concrete clean, jaws grinding. Steve bangs out of the milk house loaded with pails. The stainless steel looks ancient, not because it is old but because metal that heavy, that mirrored, has disappeared, it seems, from the world. Paper towels sprout from his pockets. He takes one out, dips it in some warm water, swings in under a cow and washes the bag. He does that two more times, a new towel each time. He has three floor milkers. He stands up, lights a cigarette, throws each towel in the gutter behind the cows. I am setting up the scale. The jazz comes over the radio. In the minute or so it will take the cows to let down the milk, Steve will go over to the room off the milk house and turn on the vacuum. The engine drowns out the radio with its own music.

I have been to Steve's farm enough to know some of the routine. I know enough to know that as I type this, since it is 11:00 P.M., Steve is beginning work on the midnight milking. It is the weekend the country goes back to sun time from savings time. When I see Steve again I'll have to ask him about his schedules and what happened this weekend. I like to be able to picture him working. It is a habit I've grown fond of. Steve milking in his barn at midnight.

In the newspaper, I just read that the passenger trains all stop and wait for the time to catch up. All those stalled trains out on the dark sidings—think of that. But it isn't the habit of habit I am thinking about tonight. Every gesture is regulated on a dairy farm. When I am up there, each cow usually gives a few pounds of milk fewer because my presence throws off the rhythm. No, routine is a given. That is one thing that makes a dairy attractive, gives the whole business its strength. Instead I am thinking about the engine that drives it all, the vacuum.

The vacuum pipe runs around the barn, circles over the stalls like a halo. It drives the claw milker, sucks the milk from the teat and draws it into the pail. As Steve switches the claw from a full pail to an empty one, his hands flit from valve to valve releasing a seal here, a pneumatic sigh, resealing. Here is atmosphere. Here is absence. After he assembles the claw and new pail, he taps back on to the vacuum line. The pail is connected by a hose. He holds the claw in his hand beneath the udder. The four teat cups and their hoses splay out and spill out of his palm. He takes up one of the far cups and slides it on the teat. At the same time, he presses a trigger on the claw and the vacuum is there. Each cup defies gravity, holds on, begins milking. There is a clear plastic bowl where the hoses meet. It turns white with milk. The milk goes in spurts from this bowl through another bigger hose into the empty pail. I carry one of the full pails up to the scale, weigh it, record the weight on another paper towel tacked to the barn wall. I subtract ten pounds for the pail. I dump the milk into a transfer unit. It is a little bigger than a kitchen wastebasket and even has a foot pedal that, when pressed, lifts and swivels the lid out of my way. Inside, at the bottom, there is a white plastic ball. It is covering the drain, keeping the air from being sucked into the system. When I pour the milk in, the ball spins and slips. The vacuum lets the ball go. It shoots up through the milk, breaches and bobs. The milk peels from it in sheets as the ball floats, then sinks with the milk rushing down the drain and into the bulk tank. The ball comes to rest in the bottom again, a big bubble in the foam.

It is never quite a vacuum, of course, because the milk is always there. The vacuum gives the milk eyes. It is the light ahead in the tunnel of tube or hose. It is what nature abhors.

But nature isn't fleeing. Steve's barn is plumbed with glass and clear plastic. I can watch the milk rush after an invisible something that retreats ahead of it. All of a sudden the pipes are flushed with white, pulsing, filling. A strange thing to say then, that nature abhors a vacuum. Maybe better to say it is consumed by it or consumes it. To see Steve's barn course with milk, though, I allow for such pathetic fallacies. Milk is animate, acts as if it lives and thinks. As it runs through the pipes, the milk seems propelled by a consciousness that might even be desire. The vacuum makes the milk come alive. Ah, this is a dairy barn, and it is easy to personify. Steve coos to the cows, fluffs a matted tail. Yes, the engine *purrs*. The pumps *whisper*. In this pause you can feel your own diaphragm contract, expand, leaving that deep hollow. The rich air of the night and the barn finds you, finds its way into you before you know it.

. . . .

I spent Labor Day weekend on Steve's farm. After the midnight milking, at two in the morning, we sat in the dooryard and looked south into the night. Steve told me again about the train because he knew I liked to hear about trains. There had been a line nearby, but it has since been abandoned. When he was a boy and milking at night, he would emerge from the barn and see the creamy lights of the passenger train streaming by. He said he guessed he imagined then the places that train was bound for. At least he conjured up, for a moment, people hidden inside the white smear of light.

Up above us there was another schedule. I hope if Haley's Comet, recently departed, did anything, it brought people out to the country to see the sky. People say that city lights wash out the light of the stars and hide the sky, as if they really know what that means. Light is as prevalent as plastic. If a stainless steel pail can surprise me, so can these stars. We sat in the lawn chairs. Steve popped open another beer. Another vacuum. Another escape. Stars fell out of the sky. One would have been enough.

As I think of it now, we talked about our weaknesses. We were clothed in the darkness and a little drunk and tired. How I hated being weak. That was my confession. We had tried to put up hay that day, and the bales were wet. I could lift them off the ground but couldn't muster enough strength to pitch them up onto the rack. Steve—Steve worried loneliness. It was a little puzzle. He only felt it after people had come to visit. After they were gone, after a few days, he didn't notice he was alone again. But friends visited because they thought he needed the company. He wanted them to come but hated the loneliness they brought with them and left behind. He found it curious that he didn't miss people more. That feeling kind of scared him.

It was a wonderful conversation that contained all kinds of emptiness. The silences of one who really is getting out of the habit of speaking. The natural pauses. The silence of not knowing what to say. The desire to say nothing that will fill up the silence. It was the talk of people who knew they should be sleeping and say only enough to keep the conversation going. Above us, that night, I like to think the sky was expanding.

It is easy thinking of Steve there. It is after milking now. Maybe he's bedded down in the barn in the new straw he has just finished pitching around. It's raining. Why run through it to the house? He'll keep the cows in. The cows are folded up on the floor, busy with the hay and chewing. The gutters are cleaned. He has spread a sandy lime on the concrete. From his bed he looks out the back door of the barn. It is a little speck of a farm, eighty acres, surrounded by huge row crop grain fields. Too easy to say it is loneliness. Too easy to say he is alone. There is the rat he hasn't been able to kill. Maybe this rat comes skipping quickly now over his outstretched legs. No, what is missing is my understanding how it really feels to be there. His life, like the night sky, cannot be fathomed. I miss getting it down right. I am missing.

. . . .

The cows stand on the highest part of the farm in a green clover field. Their color is a kind of dazzleflage, black and white, that makes it hard to judge their size or distance or even their speed when they move. The Holstein does not blend in but stands out. Still it is hard to put the whole cow together. Her black and white pieces seem to move independently of each other. Smoke dissipating. Clouds billowing. These animals are projective tests. You see things in them. Maps. Portraits. Even the outlines of cuts of meat. What is the figure? What is the ground?

The pup, Brett, bounds ahead of us, anxious to show us she can herd. A cow lowers her big head and the dog wheels, nips back over a shoulder, and runs. She goes barreling by us, back to the barn. Steve knows he shouldn't be milking Holsteins. They eat too much. Their milk just adds to the surplus. But he likes the way they look, out on the green field. As he walks up the lane, he never takes his eyes from them. "Come, boss. Come, boss," he chants. He likes the way they look. They stir as he calls, and I see an abstract shape peel from one animal then paste itself to another she is passing. A blotch from Jane splashes onto Betty who cranes to lick her flank from black to white. "Come, boss." And the cows do start flowing like the milk in the barn. It is a code of pulsing white and flashing black.

There has been so much to do this summer. Steve hasn't been able to keep current the drawings in his herd book. Ideally, he would enter all the information as soon as the calf is born. I don't trust this. I swear the white spot on the nose of a calf named Theresa moved during the summer as she grew. Steve laughs and looks through pictures of my other visits for evidence. If the book were up to date, her markings on both her sides and on her head would have been sketched in. Each page has these generic outlines of a cow. There is a lightly printed grid to help re-create the shapes. The cows that have been entered in the book haven't been finished. Lines squiggle around but no blocks of black. When I see this, the colorer in me wants to fill in, turn a pencil on its side and make the broad flat shading strokes. I want to outline, define. But I don't know the herd that well and could easily produce a pack of negative cows, an anti-herd.

The markings of these animals are abstract and are abstractly the embodiment of the vacuum. It is as if the huge sides of these creatures are chalkboards for this lesson. The world of the farm is reduced to this binary instruction. It's the physics of the farm. Their coats dumbly strobe. Here is nothing. Here is everything.

There is the white milk and the black night sky. The farm as I think about it seems to be sucked up into the realm of pure thought. The farm is real enough—the mud, the gutters. The vacuum just moves milk from point A to point B. But there is also the idea that these black and white Holsteins eerily suggest, spooky ghosts from those platonic pastures. Maybe that is what Steve is being drawn into as he drinks in his cows with his eyes. He likes the way they look. I am drawn to the whiteness of this once empty paper now swimming with black ink.

WHY THE WINDMILL?

What does that windmill mean? It is over Grant Wood's left shoulder in one of his self-portraits. Beyond, in arcs of green, is the sine curve of landscape, the equation Wood laid over eastern Iowa, his signature. The horizon, almost halfway up the picture, cuts behind the artist at mouth level, informing the shape of his lips and, by extension, suggesting the look of the midwestern face. That Gothic stare is an imprint of the land looking back. That same horizon goes on to intersect the windmill tower at the second tier. The windmill introduces a new category. The windmill bleeds off the edge of the picture. The image becomes abstract lines and *X*s. Towers are narrower at the top. All the lines conspire to create another symmetry, a vanishing point somewhere in the brown clouds, but end in an eight-petaled, half sweep of the wheel, the vane forking back to the artist's massive brow, the staring eyes behind the round glasses. Every hair on the artist's head is rendered, but the windmill, in the middle distance, is smoky, gestural. An illusion is created as the tower climbs. The windmill seems to project from the broad field of the artist's forehead a thought. But what thought?

A friend who grew up on a farm told me she was warned repeatedly when she was a child not to climb the windmill. The result, of course, was that she couldn't wait to try it. Think about children who grew up on farms when farms had windmills. I imagine them looking out over the fields by looking through the slowly cranking blades of the windmill. There is nothing moving, but the strobing blades could be the frames of a film slightly out of synch, a home movie where no one moves but the picture flickers. There is the wind, sure. When I first moved here I was told that there was nothing to slow it down after it came howling from the Rockies. And the wind made the country perfect for the mills, before electricity, to pump water from the wells for the house, the barn. The tiny platform at the top of the windmill often was the highest point on the farm. Perhaps it was the only vantage point from which to see the farm. Today airplanes are flying over all the time taking pictures. Salesmen show up later at the farms with glossies to sell. They point out to the farmers how they have gotten the angle right to hide the trash pit behind the stand of trees. Often you can't tell the order of the land until you take to the air. There, maybe, it all makes sense, lines look straight and rows neat and clean. Or maybe you can see for the first time over that last hill to the county road and beyond. At that moment your parents are turning off the blacktop onto the dirt lane heading home.

In Grant Wood's painting of Herbert Hoover's birthplace, the perspective is that of the windmill. You are on the platform looking down. And it isn't just that painting. Often he lifts you up above the farms and fields so he can put those wrinkles in a wide flat sweep of ground. And it isn't just Grant Wood who is climbing. And it's not just windmills being climbed. There are the silos, the elevators on the railway sidings, and the water towers in towns. It would not be the Midwest if there weren't this iconography of the horizontal lines punctuated by a few rickety stabs at the sky. When the ground is everywhere, it is thrilling to float for a moment above it, to see how truly it spreads out, suspended between the land and the mirroring flat-bottomed clouds. Iowa, after all, is not simply the "corn state." It is the "*tall* corn state."

What does the windmill mean there over the left shoulder of the television news anchor? Often when the nightly broadcast turns to the chronic crisis on the farm, a windmill appears hovering in the chroma-key blue sky behind the talking head. Sometimes it is part of a farm silhouette—barn and silo and bloom of windmill. Seconds count in this business. The image is shorthand. You see the windmill and you know to think *farm*. Perhaps you begin to hear its crippled creaking in a hot wind, the skeleton of the vane swinging and flapping. The grass has been growing up the buckling tower and from the road as you roar by, for a second, it looks as if the weeds and vines are pulling the whole mess down. There is no one left on the place to take care of it. The tone has been set. A few seconds, maybe a minute, is doled out on "the farm." The windmill is wiped from the screen, leaving that electric blue sky, the segue to the next graphic.

It is not only that the windmill is a vertical structure in a horizontal setting that makes it such a powerful and useful image. Nor is it simply its kinetic nature, though that is part of it. The emotional punch to watching a steam locomotive is the animation of the driving rods and pistons, the billowing smoke and steam. It moves as it moves. I've seen people weep at the sight of it. So too does the working windmill wind and pivot. Standing out above the oasis of the farmstead, the windmill blades flash and tumble. From a distance, with the tower invisible, the spinning disk seems to provide its own lift, its own gravity, a tiny silver satellite at the zenith above the barn. The movement catches the eye. This country is not only wide but still. I'll say it again. The only thing moving is the wind. It is seen only in its effect as it turns the blades. The windmill moving makes the invisible visible.

What interests me is the transubstantiation when an object such as a windmill crosses over to realm of the abstract. It is no longer just standing out in a field pumping water. It begins to stand for something else. The vines of meaning and metaphor overgrow and encase the object, a kind of topiary, and then replace it altogether.

. . . .

There are not that many windmills left in Iowa. As farms have been absorbed to form larger farms, as the farmsteads were torn down, what windmills remained after electrification came down too. They were attractive nuisances after all. They are hard to maintain. There are fewer ruins of windmills too. My friend who climbed the windmills told me that old windmills were often left standing because it was so hard to fill up the well. There is so much emptiness. First, there is the deep shaft down to the sinking water table. All the water taken out. All the digging. Spoil everywhere. And now nothing is left in the neighborhood to fill it back up, not even trash to hide from the aerial eye. A big hole in the middle of a field. Sometimes I can still see the precinct of a vanished farmyard marked by rhubarb or scraggly forsythia, a pile of brush, a gap in the fence and a rusting tower, a sapling gushing up from the well. But even these sites are disappearing. This spring there was a ruckus when a renter plowed through an old graveyard of a county care facility. The plot was restored but no one had remembered that it was there in the first place. The farmer didn't even see it until he turned up a small stone. So it is with these old places. For a while you could tell how things had been. Windmills were often set up in fence rows. Chances are good if you see a lone tower in a field, that field was subdivided once. A fence, a smaller field leads to other landscapes—animals on pasture, fallow grass, oats, or orchard. As each year goes by, as the Midwest empties itself of people, it becomes harder to imagine. And then in one day it is all gone. We've barely scratched the surface.

And yet the windmill hangs on in the imagination.

. . . .

I came upon a book in the library. *A Field Guide to American Windmills* was written by T. Lindsay Baker and published by the University of Oklahoma Press in 1985. The first one hundred pages of the book are devoted to the history of the windmill in this country. It is a story of nineteenth-century practical engineering and optimism. Two big problems needed to be solved in order to pump water for people, livestock, and steam engines. The first had to do with making the mill self-regulating, a way to shut itself off before the wind of the plains ripped up the pumping machinery. The wheel would spin out of control. This was solved in various ways through configurations of vanes and weights and springs. Perhaps the most startling innovation was employed on the early wooden models. As the wind blows harder, sections of the wheel give way like trap doors. The solid wheel turns into a rotating cylinder and, as the sections pivot out of the wind, the wheel slows. Often on the more familiar and newer metal windmills, the vane is made to swing into the wind. The wheel, with the aid of springs or weights, sets at an angle to the vane depending on the wind speed. The second problem had to do with maintenance. The invention of the oil reservoir to bathe the machinery silenced for longer, livable periods the windmill's squeaking.

The book is also a history of a technology. Such histories are always interesting because they record the industry, the energy of people and money spent on an enterprise that seems today to be completely irrelevant. It is a season of a paradigm brought to an end by cheap electricity. Such histories always allow me to daydream about the disappearance of other technologies—say computers or rifles—that seem now to be irreplaceable. Reading the histories of machines makes you imagine the world without that machine at the same time you must imagine something new to take its place.

The world of windmills is gone or almost gone. The 500 remaining pages in the book are devoted to just what the title says: a field guide. There are silhouette drawings of hundreds of windmills. Occasionally next to the large drawing there is an alternate detail, a subspecies—a vane with a colored edging or shape. The Star Model 12 had either a bold star or a stencilled *Kendallville Ind* on the sheet metal. There is a text with particulars—history and range, identifying marks, and remarks on governing and oiling. On each facing page is a photo, often taken by the author, of an example in the field. Some pictures show the windmills in a state of decay, but many have been restored or are working, especially in the Southwest where the size of the grazing ranges still makes it impractical to electrify the pumps. The names are wonderful: Daisy, Dandy, OK, Peerless, Snow (all made by the Challenge Company), Ideal, Zephyr, Maud S, Easy, Hummer, Tip Top, Whizz, Hoosier, Climax, Bright, Swift, New Era, Defender, Steel Toledo, Running in Oil Giant, Yankee, Ben Franklin, Globe, Umbrella, Swords and Surprise. They were named for the manufacturers, for places, descriptive names. Still, in the appendix there are thousands more without names or even model numbers. These are simply listed as unidentified.

I took the book with me on a trip into the country this spring. I traveled a favorite road, E-66, which cuts south and west off US 30, hugging the northern crest of the Iowa River valley. The road leads to Belle Plaine, and it is a beautiful broad plain with the greenbelt of the river appearing suddenly by the road then meandering far away to the south. The farms are scattered along the hill ridge looking out on the bottomland and the fields. Someone who lived around here once made elaborate trellises for the barns and sheds. I saw several windmills but they were all Aermotors, models from the forties and fifties. Aermotors are the sparrows of windmills. The chances are every other windmill you see in the wild is an Aermotor. On the vane is a swooshing metal brace similar to the trademark Nike puts on its running shoes. The word *Aermotor* is printed to look as if it undulates, giving the sheet metal a fluidity. They still are made, until recently only in Argentina, where a licensee sold the home company the parts, but now again from a plant in Conway, Arkansas. According to "Harness the Wind," the catalogue of the O'Brock Windmill Distributors of North Benton, Ohio, a six-foot Aermotor with tower and pumping hardware would cost a little over $2,000 and handle a shallow well or spring when erected on a hill with no wind obstructions. The Aermotors I saw were not working, but had survived, some in fine condition. One still had the governing spring intact.

I had hoped to spot more windmills or, at least, some different kinds. I saw sparrows tumble from the towers, chickadees working the scrub, jays and robins nesting in the tower webbing. I'd brought the wrong field guide and missed naming the other birds, the brown ones and the gray ones. And even the white seabirds coasting down the valley south to the reservoir near Iowa City and even further to the big Mississippi basin flew by nameless. The guide to windmills is a great book, but it is part of the machinery of transformation. Baker mentions how restoration efforts on wooden, vaneless mills are being hampered by antique collectors who pilfer the decorative counterweights of stars and roosters and bulls. The book itself, though its stated purpose is to celebrate the utility of these machines, objectifies them instead. Many of the windmills pictured in the books are restored by windmill collectors who have a crop of them scattered in a pasture, spinning and humming, milling the wind. Things of beauty. They are the ultimate lawn ornament. That is what *A Field Guide to American Windmills* is really about: the conversion of the device to art, the definition of its aesthetic. I had a classics professor once who said he knew that Structuralism was dead as a way of looking at texts because it was showing up in his journals. The soul has gone out of this machine. Skeletons are left to pick over. If we ever need windmills again to power pumps or grind feed, chances are very good we will reinvent the wheel before we refer to Baker's book.

I think the windmill is not a symbol in itself. I think the windmill does not symbolize the farms as much as it symbolizes in a precise way what we want the farm to symbolize.

. . . .

Another picture. This time it is a drawing on the dust jacket of Elizabeth Bishop's *Collected Poems.* It is a drawing of a Mexican town done by the author in 1942. In it I count forty-four American-pattern windmills of various models and makes and heights. They are all working, since the vanes are angled to the same degree. The wind is blowing at the artist's back. She is standing, at windmill level, on a balcony, looking down on the town. Below there are wires. There is electricity. But a forest of windmills sprouts above the palm trees, some as tall as the cathedral spires. It is a magical scene.

One summer, I was at treetop level flying into Greece, when the plane dipped into its glide, and at that moment there were hundreds of mirrored reflections from the flat roofs of Athens. That second, the sun had caught the solar collectors on each roof. The city disappeared in brilliant winking light.

The electrical wire connected the farm to a grid, a manifestation of the farm's growing dependence on the larger world. The farm was connected, caught up in a network. Windmills in a city, individual power plants on each home, look incongruous to a North American. The windmill means what we'd like the farm to mean. It represents the independence—self-sustaining, self-generating life. A city is the exact opposite to us. There, everything is connected by wires and pipes, hot and cold running everything, a different type of utility. Baker in his book mentions that the ranchers in the Southwest resisted the switch from wood to metal windmills because they could repair the wood ones with things on hand—nails, bolts, rawhide. To them, even steel windmills might place the farmer at a disadvantage. The idea was to remain disentangled from the wires of the world.

Of course the farms were always connected. The farmers who use windmills still, the Amish, are closely knit. But those connections, the connections of the windmill, are invisible, made of air and not run through meters. The windmill stands for the solitary worker, the resourceful American farm. Still turning, the windmill means that the whole machinery of myth is still turning.

. . . .

In Belle Plaine the old men were putting out their gardens. Their backyards could have been painted by Grant Wood. The white siding of the houses met the green lawns. The gardens were staked and strung. All those horizontal lines. And each black square of ground had a tin windmill on a tower only slightly taller than a man. When the breeze let up, the wheels let off their mad whirring and craned back and forth as if sniffing for wind.

STORIES WE TELL OURSELVES

I grew up in a high school English class. I mean this literally. My mother taught freshman English at Central High School in Fort Wayne, and one of my earliest memories is sitting at a big wooden desk by the door and listening to my mother tell stories about the stories she taught.

My mother is fond of repeating that she had me in August and by the beginning of the next semester in January she was back in the classroom. Her mother babysat me from then on, and as soon as I toddled I rode with my grandma downtown to pick up my mother at school. As a preschooler I got to go in and fetch my mother, and I wandered the huge locker lined halls. I would burst into my mother's room where she would be erasing the board or lining up the desks. The scale of the high school then was the exact opposite of what I experience now, back-to-schooling in my five-year-old's classroom, perching on those tiny chairs. Everything was huge, perhaps doubly so since Central was an old Beaux Art box with high ceilings and ornate fixtures. Mom taught on the third floor in a corner room that looked out across Barr Street at the massive St. Paul's Lutheran church and school. Its bells were geared to Westminster chimes, and as I watched my mother teach she seemed to pace her presentation to pause in time with the ringing of the bells. The pigeons always startled from the window sills, a cloud of them wafting around the spire. My mother and her students waited through the bonging, then picked up where they had left off, drilling gerunds or talking about *Silas Marner*.

Many days my mother would simply take me to school with her. My father would drop us off in the dark. Through the day, I would sit at my desk and draw or look at the pictures in the Golden Book encyclopedia I was now collecting from the supermarket, half-listening to the buzz of the classroom. I soon realized my mother was saying the same things to each new class, but each time, she presented the material as if it was completely new. In the late summers before classes resumed she would read to me as she prepared her lesson plans. *Romeo and Juliet*, *Great Expectations*, "The Necklace." To this day one of our inside jokes is a line from *Our Town*. "Mother," I will say echoing our little drama from the time I was five, "am I pretty, Mama, am I really pretty?"

After I started going to my own school, Mother would sometimes let me cut (don't tell) and come with her to Central. On days there were pep sessions I sat with her homeroom and cheered in the stands. As I learned to print, I helped her record grades, blocking in the letters in her grade book, whose perforated half-pages always amazed me. But most amazing, I was the lucky boy who ultimately received all the projects my mother's students made. I got the sugar-cubed Walls of Troy. I got the tin-foiled cardboard breastplate of Achilles. I got the toothpick longboats of Odysseus. All of these crafted Popsicle sticks and toilet-paper rolls came to me by default as her students failed to pick them up at the end of the term. My bedroom was crammed with collages and pastels, maps and charts, models of temples, the great globe itself twirling on a string from the ceiling.

. . . .

I am forty years old, and I have spent most of my life, year in year out, in a classroom. First I was a student, and now I am a teacher. What have I learned?

Well, beginning with my time in my mother's literature class I learned that the classroom was the place to read and appreciate a particular kind of art called literature. I always liked the stories my mother taught. I took to this kind of art. But I also sensed that my mother, through her alchemy as a teacher, was able to "bring to life," as we say, narratives such as *Wuthering Heights*, *David Copperfield*, *Huckleberry Finn*, and *Jane Eyre* to her students, who were economically, historically, and culturally far removed from the particulars of those books. I imagine those who teach literature continue this struggle to transmit to students the codes that will allow them to participate in, to translate, actually, these things called novels or poems or short stories and to go on then and perhaps compose their own. And this is being done in a very difficult time, for not only are these traditional forms of narration competing with other newer narrative delivery devices—movies, television, comic books, twelve-step programs—but they are also being faced with the anxiety of late-century existential questions as well.

We now know that much of the twentieth century has been about aboutness. All forms of certainty and authority have been called into question. Hierarchies, canons, and curricula are all in play, all being questioned. At the college where I teach it is quite easy now to complete a degree in English without having read a novel, short story, or poem. We joke that our students can deconstruct the Graduate Record Exam, that is, critique it historically, philosophically, politically, but they cannot pass it. No clucking of tongues or shaking of heads over this matter. I simply rehearse it here to remind myself that these are the obvious professional interests of the English classroom. It has presented and always will present a subject matter formally, be it Bob Dylan, Charles Dickens, or Jacques Derrida.

But I want to talk about the English classroom as a place itself, a site where stories happen and where they are created, not just where they are presented, appreciated, and consumed. I realized while sitting in my mother's classroom that it itself would make a great story. And so I repeated it above. The Westminster chimes, the crash of pigeon wings, the students stumbling through their memorized sonnets, my mother clapping chalk dust from her hands, a little boy sitting in the corner drawing cyclops after cyclops with his crayons.

I like the part in the *Odyssey* as Odysseus and his men make their escape from Polyphemus, the cyclops. Odysseus almost blows it once again. He has told the giant earlier that his name is "Noman." This clever lie confuses the neighbors when the wounded giant has called them for help. "No man has done this to me," etc. But in the last leg of the escape, Odysseus calls out, "Polyphemus, when you are asked who blinded you tell them it was Odysseus, son of Laertes, of Ithaca" etc. etc. Big rock, close call.

I marvel at the confidence of the hero's boast more than the wiliness of the alias, and I always imagine that years later the cyclops in his cups would be telling a friend that Odysseus, son of Laertes, of Ithaca, did this, and his companion responds, "So, who's he?" This scenario doesn't occur to our boy from Ithaca. He wants to get the facts straight. He wants his name in the story.

I teach a course in contemporary rural and agricultural literature, and I was doing so at Iowa State University, where most of the fifty students attending my class had grown up on farms or in small towns. This is nothing special. It was just the demographics of the college.

A student asked one day why we were studying these books about hog farmers and dairymen in places like Iowa and Indiana. Existential questions again. I asked her what she thought we *should* be studying. And she said, and this is true, "Well, something important, something like Greek mythology."

I said, "Okay, let's study Greek mythology. Odysseus has been away from home for twenty years. He has just hit town. He has to overthrow the suitors. Needs to lay low while he plots. Where does he go to hide out?" A long pause. "To his oldest friend, the swineherd."

The kids from the pig farms laugh. "Odysseus's dog, by the way, almost blows his cover," I continue. "We find the animal lounging where? That's right, on the dung heap."

These Iowans know the smell of manure, of course. They have been scraping the shit from the gutters of their own barns as diligently if not as heroically as any Hercules.

. . . .

Every patch of ground has its stories. The world is old, and people, the animals who tell stories, have been everywhere upon it now. The documents we use to transfer a patch of ground as property suggest this as we call them titles and deeds. Some places seem more storied than others. You are riding a bus in Greece, on the island of Evia. You rush by a rocky plain the size of a football field, one of the few open places you've seen. You think to yourself, this must have been the site of a battle, and, sure enough, upon consulting your *Blue Guide* you discover there were eight skirmishes there in the Hellenistic period alone. In Greece it is nearly impossible to build anything new because so much archaeology needs to be done first. There are all these layers to live with. And the modern Greeks, believe me, get pretty tired of watching where they step. But my point is all places contain such layers. All that is needed is a *Blue Guide* to narrate the place.

I was once helping a farmer during planting season. This was in Turin, Iowa, a place named Turin because the hills there reminded a one-word storyteller of the Italian hills. And those hills, loess hills, are composed of windblown glacial till. As a geological feature, loess hills exist in only two places in the world: in China and in western Iowa. A special place but one rather unsung, and I am sitting on a red tractor there vibrashanking the soil while the farmer is feverishly planting corn a few rows behind me. I stall the tractor. The farmer's son, discing in the next field over, sees my plight. I can't get the tractor out of gear to start it up again. He comes rushing to my aid by finding a raft and poling across the ditch flooded with spring runoff. This was years ago, but this summer when I visited that place again, Eric, the son, says, as I knew he would, "Remember that time when you stalled the tractor, and Dad was bearing down on you, and I found the raft and pole." And I do remember.

All of this happened on a field called Cottonwood, another one-word story remembering the trees that had been there once and are still there in the name of the place. I exist and my exploits exist as long as Eric tells the story. And now, you, like the recipient of a virus, know of another patch of ground because I have told you of the loess hills of Iowa, of Turin, a field called Cottonwood, a young man named Eric who at this moment is probably harvesting the corn in that field, listening to the cab radio and remembering the time he went to help an awkward city slicker named Michael. You are infected now by that mosaic chip of information, that bit of DNA that begins to replicate in you the details of a story, and you'll go home and find that you have this story to tell your family, your students, other hosts for the infection, this story about storytelling.

It was I, Odysseus, son of Laertes, of Ithaca. When you tell the story of what happened here, Polyphemus, say it was I, Odysseus, of Ithaca, son of Laertes, who blinded you. Look, I can see Eric floating on his raft calling to me.

The stories of the heroic age of ancient Greece, the ones we have studied, that have survived in our literature, that have crept into our modern pathology as "narcissism" and "oedipal," those stories were told originally by a bunch of farmers and fishermen, weavers and wine merchants perched on the rubble of rocky peninsulas and islands in the backwater of the then known world. But they took themselves and their stories very seriously.

. . . .

Mythology by Edith Hamilton was another book my mother prepped each year. I remember the wonderful line drawings inside. On the cover was the picture of the bronze Perseus holding his bent sword in one hand and Medusa's head in the other. It was the Mentor paperback edition trimmed in bronze piping. Here the stories of the classical mythologies were glossed, and my mother read to me about the flying horses, the monsters, and the gods. But even then, I realize now, I was most taken with the people who seemed, well, so like people. I am Odysseus, son of Laertes, of Ithaca. And his wife, Penelope, who undid her patient weaving and who attempted to trick her trickster husband with the riddle of their bed. And later in my own freshman English class we used Hamilton's book. The author's picture on the back, a cloudy black-and-white head shot that smacks of the studio pose of the thirties, her hair done up in a cloud of gray, her skin glossy. She looked just like Miss Colchin, my teacher, who was fond of telling us that when she had been a little girl she had sat on James Whitcomb Riley's lap. That is, Edith Hamilton looked like the schoolmarm she was, retired headmistress of Bryn Mawr School and now the great popularizer of the ancient classics.

. . . .

Think about it. How do I know, how does anyone know the ancient Greek classics? As far as I knew the lady wrote them herself, made them up on her own. Then I noticed that her brief biography also mentions her childhood in a place called Fort Wayne, the very place where I was spending my own childhood and the place where I sat studying the stories of a bunch of long-dead braggarts and blowhards. But wait, there is more. Walking home from Franklin Junior High School I would cut through Hamilton Park, cross Alice Street and Archer, then Edith Avenue. Not only did I grow up in the same city as Edith Hamilton, I actually grew up on land that had once been owned by her family. It was long thought that my school had been named in honor of Benjamin Franklin. Its yearbook was called the *Kite and Key* and its newspaper, where as an investigative reporter I broke this story, was called the *Post* as in the *Saturday Evening Post.* I discovered that my school had been named after its Franklin Street address, and that Franklin had not been Ben but Frank Hamilton. The surrounding street names all bore the names of the other brothers and sisters.

. . . .

In 1957, Edith Hamilton, at ninety, was made an honorary citizen of Athens, Greece. The ceremony took place in Athens, before a performance of the *Prometheus,* using her translation, in the Herodes Atticus, the huge amphitheater nestled beneath the Acropolis. The Parthenon and the Temple of Zeus had been lit at night before but in her honor the Athenians lit the Stoa for the first time in history. She spoke to the hillside full of people and then her version of Aeschylus's play was staged. As a bookish ninth grader raised on all this heroic stuff, I thought this was pretty cool.

And the paradox was not lost upon me. It was not just cool that someone from my hometown had gotten a bit of fame, had talked to the king of Greece and gotten a free trip to Athens. We all have general boosterish feelings when we realize that some soap star or golf pro hails from our town. As the recent play and movie remind us, we are all but six degrees of separation away from each other and so perhaps all of us are only a hop, skip, and jump away from someone with a modicum of fame or notoriety. No, in thinking about Edith Hamilton the gushing adulation I felt was of another order. It had to do with authoring and creating. You see, Hamilton herself, through her writing, had inscribed in me the very notions about fame and famous deeds that now swelled my breast. That is, for me she was a kind of metacelebrity, for in order to understand celebrity itself I had to digest the great stories of heroes she, Edith, had composed. It is as if Hamilton was the wizard from Kansas. Do not pay any attention to the man behind the curtain. A girl from Fort Wayne, Indiana, had in a very real sense kept the civilization of ancient Greece alive, not by doing the chores of Hercules or by defeating the Trojans in battle but by writing about those heroes and deeds. She was epic in a self-effacing way. She was essentially invisible, the medium of transmission. And to me this is a great story.

. . . .

Hamilton Park, where I played, had once been a trash dump, a hole dug deep in the ground and filled with rubbish, the refuse heaps not quite reaching the lips of the embankments that surround it. Now it is a grassed over crater. When I played there as a child I loved the days after it rained because on those days the junk that had been buried beneath the ball diamonds and picnic tables would work its way to the surface. I found old blue medicine bottles and pearl buttons, tin cans and bed springs. Sometimes whole tires would appear overnight in the middle of the football field, or while sliding into second your spikes would slice open a burrow of coiled hose. There were hummocks of eroding books too, the weathered pages like geological strata. And once the door of an icebox emerged near the scoreboard. You could open it, and it was like opening a tomb, a hatchway underground or back in time. The grassy banks around the park, I used to imagine, must be like the hillsides of Greece—Epidaurus, Dodoni, and even the cliff of the Acropolis where the Herodes Atticus was carved out. I thought of my playground as a theater, as a stage, and as a kind of automatic archaeology with the history of this place, the old used mechanisms of its working, its gears and balance wheels, its urns and amphora bubbling up at my feet.

. . . .

Mythology, of course, was a religion for ancient peoples and though we are reminded of that by the dutiful teachers and in prefaces to collections of stories, it is hard for us to imagine these tales as such. They come to us in literature classes as beautiful vessels, shells of cicada, and we admire them for their aesthetic power, perhaps for some of their ethical lessons but mainly I think it is odd to us that people found in this set of stories an immense system of belief. Of course our religious nature has been tutored by another set of stories. Though certainly stirring and equally compelling, the episodes of the Bible don't strike us the same way. One big reason has to do with point of view. The gods in ancient mythology did not write the text of the religion. Its writers, though perhaps inspired by gods through the muses, treat the deities as characters and actors. The Bible, especially the Christian testament, strikes us as more rhetorical, its stories are illustrative of the revealed word of God. To the Greeks, I think, the telling of the story itself was the religious act. Their church, after all, was a theater. There they listened to the retelling of a vast structure of connections. Their stories were all happening simultaneously. Theseus knew Oedipus, palled around with Heracles. They were related. They intermarried. The gods were everywhere too. And this all had taken place only a few generations before, say about the time of our Civil War, and the deeds were over, the heroes all dead in about a generation's time. The Bible reads more sequentially. After all, its great purpose is linear, to record and predict the one big story of God's drama with his creation. The stories were over in mythology. There is no revelation and no apocalypse. In the world of the Bible, we live in the middle of a great unfinished narrative and we are waiting for and participating in its ending. The Greeks lived within a labyrinth of stories, of finished tales whose intricate structure promises infinite variation.

. . . .

I went to graduate school at Johns Hopkins University in the late seventies. Hopkins is known for its medical institutions but it maintains a small liberal arts and sciences campus and is the site of the first graduate schools of the humanities and sciences. I went there to study writing. I had never been outside of Indiana before, while most of my colleagues were easterners fresh out of Ivy League schools. As I have said, I learned my lessons well, and my first efforts at writing stories were derivations of the stories I had read in other classrooms. It was after class in the Grad Club, where we debriefed over beers and fried food, that I related the more or less true stories of Indiana. My listeners were well traveled but knew far more about Europe, England, and even India than they knew about Indiana. Indiana to them was as remote as the planet Mingo, and it was then partially in response to their response, partially as an expression of homesickness, and mainly as an application of my understanding of mythology that I began writing stories about Indiana.

When I wasn't writing stories I would wander the campus and make myself a nuisance in the biology labs. In the late seventies, the revolution in genetic engineering was just getting started. The technique of snipping genes with certain enzymes and pasting them onto the chromosomes of another had just been patented, and the graduate students in the biosciences practiced doing that, snipping and pasting DNA, as if they were practicing scales. I had a friend named Eric, another Eric, who worked in the labs and one day pulled out a tray of slides to show me. See, he said, these are *E. Coli Ericson.* He told me he had attached a gene from a frog onto the bug that lives in all our guts. The smears I was looking at were a new form of life, and he named them after himself. I am Odysseus, son of Laertes, of Ithaca.

Today scientists at Hopkins are putting together the human genome map. The project began in the desire to identify the deleterious genetic material, the genes that actually cause inherited diseases, and has expanded to the incredible feat of identifying the function of all 100,000 genes packed on the twenty-three pairs of human chromosomes. An early discovery, of course, was that there are very few genes that directly cause things; however, the map reveals that there are thousands of genes that create a disposition, a likelihood of certain consequences. They have discovered the location they believe indicates an aptitude for musical ability. In my goofier moments I fantasize about the possibility of the storytelling gene. My fantasy gene is not an indicator that some of us have that gene and some of us don't. No, what I think is in there is an instruction that makes us all storytellers and makes us all hunger to hear stories.

Mythologies, whether ancient or Hoosier, seem to me to be like the human genome. Both use a limited set of building blocks, alphabets or proteins, in near infinite combinations to transmit complex collections of information, codes, and instructions. The way we have come to think of our biological inheritance is a metaphor based on storytelling. Isn't it curious that when groping for a model to explain how we reproduce we have settled on explaining it in those terms. It seems right to us to figure this apparatus of inheritance in terms of sequence, of language, of narrative, of story. And embedded in each level is the wizard behind the screen, the story gene, this disposition, this hunger for stories, almost as if our very essence is tied to the creation of story. We tell stories because we are human and we are human because we tell stories.

. . . .

Mythologies to me seem to be always local and scaled to a human size. Even the monsters, the giants, and the gods behave in ways we recognize. "I like you, Noman," says the cyclops Polyphemus to Odysseus. "I will eat you last!"

The advent of mass media—the book, newspaper, radio, television, etc.—distorts that human scale. It is easy to feel that we know the O. J. Simpson story better than we know our own stories. Locally, do you know the mil rate of your township tax assessment? Borders, always arbitrary, of one's neighborhood, city, state, country—are they even viable anymore?

The stories we tell ourselves create the very space that we as a group, any group, inhabit. Place is made by story. Recall the end of the *Odyssey* when Odysseus is instructed by the gods to hoist an oar on his shoulder and walk inland until no one recognizes the tool, until someone asks why he is carrying the winnow out of season. The true regions of the world we live in are mapped by the stories we tell.

. . . .

Mythologies are connected stories that ultimately form a cultural map of a place. I have pushed my own stories to include the space that has been known as Indiana, but those stories have tended to seep into the surrounding region. The Midwest is a good example of that kind of placeless place. But stories told about it are beginning to construct it. Where is it? My students in Iowa would not include Indiana in the Midwest. As a Hoosier, I think of Kansas and Nebraska as part of the Plains at least if not the West itself. To be a midwesterner is to begin with the justification of using that name, and what it means is still building through an interweaving of local stories. In my own case, I discovered while reading about Edith Hamilton that as she lived her final years in Washington, D.C., she took to visiting the incarcerated Ezra Pound in St. Elizabeth's Hospital there. I was writing a story about Pound, who had his first teaching job at Wabash College in Indiana, and I included Edith Hamilton as an unnamed character in my story. The current senator of the state of Indiana was in my dorm at Indiana, and my most recent project—stories narrated by Dan Quayle—began when I rediscovered a letter he wrote to me when he was my representative in Congress praising my first book of poems set in Fort Wayne. Our lives and our stories are twined together.

. . . .

Mythologies, finally, are always also about storytelling. Mythologies are presented as self-conscious of their cultural mission of mapping a place as well as mapping themselves. Recall that Odysseus himself is asked to recount his own travels to the court he is washed into after leaving Calypso. He is moved to tell his story after he has listened to a singer sing the story of the fall of Troy. Of course, mythologies are self-conscious because they acknowledge the human problem and advantage of memory itself. Recall that the mother of the Muses was Memory. And yet individually we are trapped in perceiving time sequentially. Mythology, and I keep thinking of a biological/mechanical metaphor, seeks to attach a cultural memory into our experiential wiring. Stories are viral. A good example of this is the collection of folk legends, both urban and rural, that get repeated as the truth. There are many factual inaccuracies in my Indiana stories. I am self-consciously altering the details or making up ones I do not know. In so doing the storyteller faces the existential dilemma of fact and fiction. The things we do are done. We are always left with the residue of events, evidence. And all that residue can, by definition, be manipulated and shaped for many purposes, one of which is the myth building I have been speaking of.

Myths are local, connected, and self-conscious. Tell them I am Odysseus, Laertes' son, of Ithaca. In the stories we tell ourselves, we tell ourselves.

. . . .

I noticed as I sat in my mother's classroom that from time to time she would refer to me as an example of something under discussion in the text at hand. I was Pip-like or the way I played games in the neighborhood mimicked the structure of the quest they were discussing. I had a strange feeling sitting there in my big desk as all the eyes in the class turned to the little boy in the corner. I was being read. I was a text. And at this moment, in my own text, my memory searches for a reference. I think of Elizabeth Bishop's poem "In the Waiting Room" in which she says of a similar moment, "I was an I / I was an Elizabeth." I also think of the wonderful experiments in child development where researchers daub a smudge of ashes on the foreheads of observed children. The children of several ages are playing in a room of mirrors and it is only ones of a certain age who notice their reflections and stop before the mirror. They understand that they are in the mirror and that the ash is on their foreheads and they now know to wipe it off.

I, whoever I am, am a text created in my mother's classroom. I am a lucky boy since the transmission of my biological and cultural heritage took place under such circumstances, in such close proximity. I am Michael, my mother's son, of Fort Wayne, Indiana.

ICONOGRAPHY

Indianapolis

It is midnight. On the front lawn of the church, we surround the *Kouvouklion,* the small decorated wooden table with a little dome used as a catafalque to transport the *Epitafios,* a painted cloth icon representing Christ entombed. It is midnight, and the bells of Holy Trinity Church begin to peal, starting in sets of three, as sets of three are an important part of the ritual of Orthodox faith, perhaps even more so at a church named for the Holy Trinity. The bells ring, first in threes, then exploding into ever expanding multiples, creating rippling patterns of pitch and timbre with no melody so that there is no notion of when, or if, the now cacophonous pealing will end. At the same time, Father Gounaris begins the triumphant chant, *Christos Anesti,* Christ has risen. The congregation sings with the singing priest, the lit candles we hold inscribing the sign of the cross in the air before us, a kind of musical conducting, sweeping up, then right, then left while the bells boom and the chant hits its heavy solid beats.

I am standing with my back to North Pennsylvania Street, looking back through the dome of the *Kouvouklion*, facing Father Gounaris who now begins the chant again in English:

Christ has risen
from the dead
by trampling down
death by death.

Holy Trinity Church is behind him, and my eyes follow the swing of the *Pascha* candles upward to the blue-black sky studded with stars over Indianapolis of all places. Indianapolis, whose name is a fossilized amalgam of languages and histories, misidentifications by emigrants of one people from one place with another people in another place and its epithet of fragmentary Greek, *polis*, the *city*, yes, but also the *people* in Greek, the same Greek that is now again, as the song returns to Greek, in the air over this city and these people.

On either side of the open church doors, dogwood trees are just beginning to bloom. My response to seeing the pale white buds at this moment—with the bells, the singing, the candles—is complex. At first I am surprised as I had heard from a friend here in Indianapolis that the dogwoods and redbuds were blighted this year, dying without blooming. She had told me this as I made plans for coming up from Alabama, where I live now, to this Easter service in Indianapolis. At the time I talked to her, the dogwoods and redbuds, ten hours farther south and a month before, were glorious in color. I had just moved to the South and had never seen such a spring. I grew up in Indiana, in Fort Wayne, where it was a rare spring when my grandfather, who moved from Kentucky to Fort Wayne, actually was able to coax the flowering trees into flower. It was my grandfather who always repeated each spring the legend that the wood for the cross was taken from the dogwood, that Judas hanged himself on the redbud, its crimson flower representing drops of blood.

So my discovery of the blooming dogwoods at the doorway of the church made me think of all these things, the coincidence of many narratives, and how symbols and stories are transported as people move around in the world. To me the dogwood and the redbud always seemed like southern trees, Kentucky trees, but in all of those years of my grandfather's retelling I never thought until that moment that the dogwood and the redbud might not be Mediterranean trees. Are they even native in the Holy Land? And I am thinking about the nature of the relationship, how people and what they believe are connected to the places they left and those they inhabit now. And I am thinking this on the front lawn of a Greek church a couple of blocks from 38th Street in Indianapolis, where my grandfather, joking, always insisted the South began. And on this spot, and in a foreign language, I am listening to a very old story about death being dead and thinking of my grandfather who died in the same year the dogwoods were supposed to never bloom in Indiana but did.

Sparta

I wake up, and I am in Indiana again. I see, through the windows of the bus, fields of elephant-eye-high corn. How strange! When I fell asleep I was touring the Peloponnese in Greece, riding a bus up from the ruined city of Monemvasia to Sparta. I fell asleep in the semiarid, rocky landscape to which I'd grown accustomed. Orange and olive groves, date palms and fig trees. Now this. How un-Greece-like! Rows of green tasseled corn and red tractors, prefab metal buildings and spinning windmills. Sparta itself looks like no other Greek city I have ever seen. It is platted out on a grid like a small town in the American Midwest, not the viney, overlapping lattice growth of the typical Greek city or village, whose design reaches back to the ancient memory of the Minotaur's maze on Crete and the warrens of alleyways and paths that acted as defenses against pirate attacks on the dice-white island villages spilling off mountains down to the sea. Sparta, then, is an anomaly. Built by the philhellene French in the nineteenth century on the site of the militaristic city-state of classical Greece, restored not to its former glory, as no one remembered what it looked like before the Romans leveled it and salted the earth, but to the specs of enlightened empire design. So present-day Sparta, like Indianapolis, say, is an imaginary city, one staked out and planned by fiat, not organically evolved from continuous inhabitation. This Sparta appeared overnight. And it made its appearance around the same time the American Midwest was sprouting towns. So it re-creates, in my mind, this strange association of the feel of its streets and spaces.

Consequently, Sparta isn't on the usual must-see lists. But I'm not on the usual tour. A few years before this trip, I married a Greek-American woman, Theresa, from Baltimore, and introduced her to Indiana by taking her on an extensive car trip across the state soon after we met. I like to say, half jokingly, that we honeymooned in Indiana. We stopped in Santa Claus and French Lick. We visited the almost-empty convent in Ferdinand, where the nuns showed us the vestments they had made and the tea towels on which they had embroidered the state bird. At Columbus, we walked among the architectural monuments and discovered, across from the Bartholomew County Courthouse, the turn-of-the-century soda fountain, Zaharikos, run by a Greek family. Were they from Sparta? No, perhaps that soda fountain wasn't in Columbus but was in

Princeton, Indiana, or in the candy shop in Iowa Falls, Iowa. No, it was in the one in Wilton, Iowa, the Wilton Candy Kitchen. Or it was somewhere else in the Midwest—in a coffee shop, a pizza take-out, a bar and grill—where the proprietor had a picture on the wall of Mount Tayegetos looming over Sparta, and I told him of our trip there.

This trip to Greece is Theresa's returned favor for my dragging her around Indiana. It has been cobbled together wonderfully by local buses and her facility with the language. We visit the comparable off-the-beaten-track roadside attractions of rural southern Greece. Here, in Sparta, we stumble upon this strange intersection with my home and homeland. During that late evening's *volta*, the nightly walk Greeks take before retiring, we sort out what remains in a place to create Place and what remains in our memories to create who we are. And call to mind what it is we take with us when we move from place to place as we move along amidst the Spartans, strolling, heading toward the well-lit *Zaharoplasteion* on the square for *pagato*, which you and I know as ice cream.

Indianapolis

Almost midnight and all the lights of Holy Trinity Church are being extinguished. The Orthodox service is designed as a drama with its re-creation weekly of the last supper, the crucifixion, and the resurrection. The church, I think, is very good at creating compelling productions out of very simple elements—light and shadow, bread and wine and water and oil, the few gestures of the priest.

My sons were both baptized in Greek churches, Sam at Saint Nicholas in Baltimore and Nick at Saint Sophia in Syracuse, New York. The baptism is a good example of what I mean. The babies, naked, were dunked, totally immersed, three times, of course, in the name of the Father, the Son, and the Holy Spirit, into the water of the font which had been anointed on its surface at the start with a cross of floating olive oil. At last, howling, the babies were hauled aloft by the priests. They were red, wet, dripping, oily, bawling, exactly the way they looked when they were born physically a few months before this second birth. And seeing them then, again, fierce, heaving for breath, alive, I was again at their first births and all my visceral responses kicked in once more. And that is the point—that this new birth is not just *like* birth, it *is* birth.

On *Pascha*, Easter, the weekly symbolic evocations of sacrifice and resurrection are themselves transformed, taken to an even higher intensity. Now, in this dark, the *iconostasis*, the screen which separates the nave of the church from the sanctuary, takes on a heavier weight of darkness, the wall of the tomb. Suddenly, a single candle flame erupts behind the Beautiful Gate, the center doorway of the *iconostasis*, backlighting the grillwork of the gate and defining its bulk. The flame's piercing rays seem to outline us all in the darkness of the church. With just this single light we can make out, barely, the gate being slowly opened, the stone being rolled away, the light moving toward us. And then the flame splits into two lights and then almost instantly doubles in number again and then again, moving in quick leaps left and right, streaming now from person to person back toward me in the last row to the candle I hold.

Oh, I suppose a part of me, the modern man, two thousand years after the stone was rolled away and the Light of the World appeared, sees through this ritual or, more exactly, sees it as only symbolic. That is, I could engage in it on this intellectual level, from a distance, for what it symbolizes, what it represents. The church is the mother lode of symbols and metaphors.

Everything teaches, everything represents something, everything prompts us to call to mind another time and place when the Son of God walked on earth, when the saints and martyrs evangelized and died, when heaven will be visited on earth. I understand all that because I am a user of metaphor myself. But at certain moments I forget to think and begin to feel. The metaphoric contraption works and, working, falls away, and I have been transported to these other places and times, transported into these stories and they are no longer merely stories. The Greek Church is very good at the manipulation of my senses into believing. And I do appreciate its skill because I am professionally a storyteller, a writer of fiction and drama. But, at times, I even forget to remember to note my professional self-conscious respect and admiration, I forget to remember where I am really, in Indianapolis, in Indiana, and I am at the mouth of a tomb and I hear a voice saying, "The one you are looking for is not here."

Mystras

Outside Sparta is the ruined city of Mystras, one of the important Byzantine cities along with Monemvasia and Constantinople. It is a red-brick ruin of the more recent Christian era so does not enjoy the tourist trade afforded the white marble ruins of the classical age. Theresa and I, it seems, have the place to ourselves. We wander through the acres of collapse, the piles of rubble marking the collapse of Greece into the Ottoman Empire six hundred years ago. There is, to our surprise, a working convent here. We peer through the grill of the gate and see a nun slowly sweep the flagstones of the courtyard. Surrounding the walled convent are huge piles of stone and dust, houses and shops and churches swept into huge heaps. A few of Mystras's churches have been rebuilt slowly by donations from private citizens, and some have had their interior frescoes and icons restored to their medieval splendor. There is a tiny domed Saint Michael. We stumble upon a church named for the Virgin built into the side of the mountain. There is a guard inside who is happy to see us. He warns Theresa against taking photos of the *Pantocrator* or the *Theodoxos,* frescoes of Jesus the Ruler of the Universe and Mary the Mother of God, but then he turns away, his hands entwined with *komboloi,* worry beads that he worries, I suppose, on his lonely post, and with his back turned indicates with a little flick of his fingers to go ahead and take a picture. "See," the gesture says, "I am not looking." Theresa does put her camera to her eye to focus on the Mother of God but discovers that it is too dark. Instead we stand in silence, our eyes sweeping over the walls and roof of the church, every inch of it decorated with paintings, paintings telling stories. Spontaneously, the guard starts singing, the monotonic a cappella chant of church, something from the vespers probably, perhaps just to demonstrate the acoustics of the mortar and stone but maybe because he wants to share this place with us, animate it fully so that we, in the few moments we visit, get a sense of his daily experience, a space brought back to life, in focus and in full voice.

Ames, Athens, Indianapolis

It is probably clear by now that I have lived in many places. I teach at universities so have moved from Maryland to Iowa to Massachusetts to New York to Alabama. Perhaps because I *have* moved so much, I tend to write about Indiana though I haven't lived there for years, a compensation for all my wandering. America, a nation of immigrants, has never had its own major outpouring of citizens. Its emigrations have all been internal—the farm to the city, the city to the suburb, the east to the west, the south to the north and back again. It is a great drama, community and claustrophobia on the one hand, freedom and rootlessness on the other—my one grandfather moving north out of Kentucky hauling its flora with him, my other grandfather leaving Italy and landing on Brandruff Street in Fort Wayne, Indiana, never to move again.

It is my story, of course, but America's story as well. The Greek Church's diaspora went along with the Greek people. It began from a very specific place called Greece, and its history intensely dramatizes the dilemma of identity and assimilation. How can a faith so rooted in a place make a place for itself elsewhere? Perhaps more than any other transplanted Christian faith, Greek Orthodoxy suffers the question profoundly, what with its national boundaries nearly indistinguishable with those of the church and the language. There is, moreover, the pride of that place and all that history. The Greeks, you recall, invented *hubris*. Paul, using the Greek language, proselytized, the word itself from Greek, in the Athenian *agora* within living memory of Christ's life. The Church tended the faith during the period of Ottoman hegemony by kindling the language and the ethnic identity. To be Greek and Greek Orthodox often seems seamless.

Here's a funny story, probably apocryphal. We heard it from the Greek students we met when we moved to Ames, Iowa, and Iowa State University. The fraternities there were having a huge party advertised for Greeks only. It seems a Greek student, Yanni, showed up at the gate and was told he couldn't come in. "For Greeks only," the frat brothers said. "But I am Greek!" Yanni said. "No, you're not Greek," he was told again. "I am Greek!" Yanni said, knowing it is enough just to assert this obvious truth. The Greek students telling us this story have in their telling a kind of poignancy, a sympathetic understanding of Yanni, their protagonist (a Greek word), and his inability to comprehend a Greek world not his own.

Tonight, in Indianapolis, I am Greek and I am not Greek. At the meal following the *Pascha* service I sit with five others, strangers to me until now. We introduce ourselves by playing the egg-breaking game. Earlier, we were all given the red-dyed Easter eggs as we filed out of church and into this very Hoosier gymnasium at the back of Holy Trinity to break the fast with a supper of lamb and feta and olives and *christopsomi*, the special Easter bread. We say *Christos Anesti* and tap the eggs' ends together, a kind of wishbone-breaking contest. Mine survives all challenges. The woman next to me has just converted, having married, recently, the man next to her. Her husband emigrated from Salonika as a young man. *Christos Anesti*, I say. Truly, he has risen, she says in English. Her husband is talking to his friend and his friend's wife in Greek. Something about a trick the one has played on the other convincing him that the candles this year would be replaced by flashlights. I believed him, he says, in English, laughing. This evening, Father *had* warned communicants to watch their candles so as not to set anyone's hair on fire. It made sense, he says, still laughing. The other man is Greek and doesn't speak English. He is visiting, like me. I want to ask him, but can't because of the language barrier, how different this night is from Easter back home.

We represent all the variations of this faith, I think. I tell everyone I have come from Alabama. It is three o'clock Easter morning. I feel at home but also far away from home.

The Meteora

It is as if we are on the moon. On all sides, gigantic boulders, bleached by the sun and sanded smooth by the eons of rain and wind. It is a landscape like no other I have ever seen save maybe that of the background of a Roadrunner cartoon, naked buttes and precariously balanced rocks leering over sheer cliffs with massive crags. We are walking through this valley hedged around by one-piece mountains whose name, Meteora, suggests their arrival, whole, from heaven above.

Perched on the top tip of the largest boulders are the monasteries. Only recently has the bishop here ordered the cutting in of stairs to reach them. They still have the woven baskets, lowered from the trap doors of overhanging wooden wings of the houses to the valley floor. The monks still winch up water and food and more wood and stone to continue the impossible, asymmetrical building above.

We climb the sets of thousands of stairs to see the churches and the icons, the frescoes in the rectories and the relics of the saints. On the way up we see a hermit's cave or two bored into the mountain face across the valley, a sheet of solid rock stained like a natural fresco with its own aesthetic nuance. At the top we are greeted by the monks as *xenoi*—strangers, guests, pilgrims—and offered the traditional Greek hospitality of coffee and *glika*, incredibly sweet preserves of oranges, cherries, or grapes.

In one monastery, teetering above the toy city of Kalambaka below, a young monk with Coke-bottle-bottom lenses in his eyeglasses breathlessly relates to us the wonders of his recent trip to New York, *Nea Yorki*, and the results of laser surgery there. He recalls the shadows of the tall buildings, the canyons he walked through, the observation decks of skyscrapers. All around us are the ancient painted icons with their staring eyes and the open windows of the monastery looking out on the deep blue bottomless sky.

Des Moines, Cambridge, Indianapolis

I remember. *"Signomi, Yiayia!"* Excuse me, Grandmother. An usher says this at Saint George's in Des Moines as he slides the delicate old woman down along the slick pew so that others can pack in for the service.

I remember. A teenage girl in the narthex of the Saints Constantine and Helen in Cambridge whispers with a Boston accent to her friend, "Aphrodite, let me use your hair brush."

It is hard to capture, perhaps, all that goes on during any one service. I am always taken by the juxtaposition of extreme solemnity of ritual with casual hubbub of earthbound life. As I watch, the priest and deacon and the altar boys scurry around and about the raised area in the front of the nave emerging from the sanctuary behind the iconastasis. They disappear and reappear at the north or south gates, move about sacred objects spontaneously, bustling like a janitorial crew. You see them dress and redress preparing for the great processions while all the time the chanters and choir can be singing like angels about the angels. Ushers hustle candles to the front, in ones or twos, brought to the fore to be placed beneath the various icons while latecomers light slim tapers in the open narthex in the rear of the church. The service is meant to be a dramatic re-creation of the life and death of Christ, but as a play, it is most like the self-conscious kind, *Our Town*, say, with the stage manager stopping to comment on the action and move about stage property, set the scene to come. And just now Father Gounaris does break character and directs the congregation to watch out for the candle flame when taking communion. Earlier on the front lawn of Holy Trinity I watched as he nudged a new battery into the handheld mike moments before the bells began to ring beatifically. It is like watching baseball, I think, the only sport where the ball doesn't do the scoring. You must watch the ball *and* the runners running, a wide view of the field. It is as much about the periphery as it is the pinpoint. The Greek Church is simultaneously homely and divine, human and ethereal. The priest is chanting within the sanctuary. We see him framed by the open portal of the Royal Gate. The choir is singing something else. The evening ebbs and flows. The priest is an actor and then acts as a commentator or critic of the action, explains what has happened before our eyes, what is yet to come. Suddenly we are transfixed by the great procession of the Gospel or the Gifts; the parades of transfigurations, both miraculous and routine, parade before us.

There is much anxiety surrounding the veneration of icons in the church. Church literature is at pains to explain the difference between worship and veneration, how our love is directed to the one represented and not toward the material thing of wood and paint itself. It is clear to me that the icons are windows, a kind of porous membrane separating these worlds, the corporeal and the spiritual. While the liturgy is performed, both worlds are present, these overlapping spheres of space and place, the divine and human. I attend, at the same time, all the gestures and the words, sense the music and the incense. I wait and witness the tedium of certain parts while I am transfixed by other parts. I sense the capillary attraction between these realms. The evening contains and dramatizes all of these places and creates the possibility of imagining a wholly other dimension while being deeply rooted in our own mundane one.

Indianapolis

After the supper, early in the morning, I make my way through the crowded gymnasium over to Father Gounaris to thank him for this evening. I explain to him how I got here, here to Holy Trinity, to Indianapolis, this night. How my wife is Greek from Baltimore, *Valtimori* I say. "You say that really well," Father Gounaris compliments me. I give him a thumbnail of my wandering—the churches I know in Des Moines, Cambridge, Syracuse, Birmingham. I tell him of my sons' baptisms, my trips to Greece. My whole life in a few quick gestures, blurring. I tell him what has interested me most is this dilemma of place and movement, how the Greek Church is and is not Greek. At the end of the *Pascha* service, right before the eggs and the icon cards were distributed, before we sat down to dinner, Father Gounaris stepped forward, slightly winded from the long night's festivities but jazzed and obviously joyful, to address his flock. This impromptu homily touched on this very issue. He annunciated to the assembled flock what was obvious to us all, how different we all were from one another and how all bound up together we were now in one place and time. At Holy Trinity that night there were the sons and daughters of Greeks who would never set foot in Greece, there were converts converted for all reasons, *and* there were Eritreans from Africa in their native dress, there were descendants of Serbs, Russians, Poles, Macedonians, as well as Greek Americans who left their homeland for who knows what reasons and found themselves here. It was a prayer answered, I thought, Father Gounaris recognizing the fact of our different story lines and their intersection here this night. He acknowledged this fact of faith in a few words of English, a language that will do as good as any.

THE OTHER HOUSES IN ELDON, IOWA

Iowans like to tell you that, once, you could go anywhere in the state and still never be more than ten miles from the nearest rail line. Today you are never very far away from a corridor of ruins.

Iowa has that tended look of a train set. The buildings of the small towns and farms were prefabricated, shipped in parts, ordered from catalogues, giving the landscape a generic, standardized look. Barn. House. Windmill. Water tower. Tree, even. Assorted animals. Townspeople. The scene is in a different scale.

The frontier swept through here and didn't slow down until it hit the grasslands and became the timeless frontier of farther west. Iowa was settled fast and now one hundred years later has begun to take itself apart. It seems as if the tracks have been rolled up. The abandoned roadbeds are conduits to a past this land now has, and along the route of the Rockets, the old Rock Island Railroad's Chicago to Kansas City main line, you'll see what could not be torn down, salvaged, or scrapped. Old coal bunkers. Bridge piers in the Des Moines River. Mounds of rotting ties and truckless wooden boxcars used as sheds.

I followed a section of that main line, driving through the toy farms of the Amish settlement near Bloomfield, then along J 15 through Floris toward Eldon in the southwest corner of Wapello County. My great-grandfather, who farmed in Kentucky and got out of it as soon as he could, constantly schemed. One of his ideas was to buy a right of way like the one I was tracing and plant potatoes, one long row of potatoes so he would only turn the team once. Schemes.

Here and there along the road the grassy dike ducked down to the grade of the road, crossing ahead of me. I rushed over the wake of embedded rail. The state is still in court arguing who should suffer the cost of removing these little sections of track. It will come down to who was at this crossing first, who crossed who. The crossings were guarded by the X signs, a punctuation etched in my mind for stopping, looking, listening. Further on there was a signal box, its silver paint gleaming. And then a foreshortened stand of telegraph poles sprang up in a religious grouping. When I got close enough, I saw the glass insulators had been stripped from the crossbeams by speculators. It wasn't long ago there was a market for heavy amber insulators along with the Avon bottles and Depression glass of the flea markets. No more.

I crossed into Eldon on a narrow truss bridge spanning a hearty stretch of the Des Moines River. Further downstream I could see where the rails would have crossed the climbing berm. There, on that side of the river across from the town, I could make out the smudges of the yard and shop and roundhouse foundation in with the corn. The railroad was almost everything to this town. I noticed where the two broad crossing strips of grass and cinders marked the center of Eldon. Here the other main line from Des Moines met the one from Chicago. Eldon was a division point: crews were changed, cars were classified, and engines were serviced. A little station still stood at the junction, but more memorable were the huge empty places that stretched away from it. There seemed to be reluctance to encroach upon the space. The bins of the elevator to the north straddled the curving spur. The houses to the east fronted a huge playing field. Even the trucks behind the stores on Main Street parked at contorted angles away from the widening cinder strip as if at any moment a train of hoppers would appear again or as if the ground had been sown with salt. I was going to say that the town felt gutted, but it was more like Eldon had been filleted. The bone is all out of it.

In 1930, the artist Grant Wood traveled along these same roads with a student of his, John Sharp, who was from Eldon. The story goes that Sharp wanted to show Wood a house on the town's northern edge and took him by to see it. Wood made a sketch of the house on the back of an envelope, according to what I read on the place mat at the Jones Cafe and Gothic Room. This part I question since it seems borrowed from the details surrounding Lincoln's train ride to Gettysburg, his sketch of the speech on the back of an envelope. In any case, Wood added in the final painting his sister, Nan, and his dentist, Dr. B. H. McBeeby, a pitchfork between them, in front of the house he saw on that visit. According to the place mat, he ate at the Jones Cafe. If he sat in the corner booth as I did, near the window, he would have seen the action at the junction—a panting switch engine shunting from track to track, a crowd swelling on the platforms, a semaphore signal snapping up. Eldon as a post office WPA mural, the kind Wood's students rendered in towns all over Iowa. But it would not be the bustling social realism in front of him that caught Wood's eye that day. Instead, his painting would comment on the small town by focusing on those two severe faces and the big blank window of the white house. *American Gothic*, one of the best known images in the world, has always been misread. Not a farmer and his wife but a father and daughter. Not a farmer at all but a small-town man. You can tell that by the shirt he wears, Wood said.

Yes, the railroad was almost everything to this town. I gleaned the evidence from the vertical file at the town library. Under Eldon I found rotogravure articles of last train rides, articles about boxed-lunch excursions downriver. And there were articles about the painting, with the house always in the background, the lowly capstone mention of Eldon in the newspaper formula of the inverted pyramid. While I searched the files, a painter gave estimates to the librarian. The library's spacious reading room was to be renovated. The librarian told me that this would be the first major work done on the prairie-style bungalow. She didn't want the ceiling dropped, the windows closed up. But heat was expensive. The only other patrons were a mother and son reporting on the books the boy had read this week as part of a summer contest. The librarian told me the prize was a night out in Ottumwa, movies and ice cream. Her folks had been railway people, her husband a retired conductor. She showed me the model of the Gothic House a Kenny Norris had done, a bit squat I remember, the scale not contributing to the vertical lightness of the one in the picture. I hadn't seen the real one yet. It was cool in the library, heat only a problem in the winter. The wood was old oak and polished. The etchings and tintypes of the town fathers, the ones I read about in the centennial history, blended in with the print of Wood's most famous painting on the dull white walls.

"She's supposed to be the man's daughter," the librarian said.

The librarian too shared that plain, upright look of the images, the real and imagined, on the walls around her. It was hard to read her, to interpret how she felt about her town now. I saw her as the last pilot of another elaborate vehicle of the nineteenth century, still steaming on Mr. Carnegie's assumptions of the future. She was friendly, helpful, but ultimately neutral on the subject of the town she served, dispensing and collecting information.

My trip through Eldon so far had been about space. In the library's airy hall, the tintype images revealed men with their heads held rigid by braces when they posed while their images burned into metal. I thought of sacred icons. Icons are screens between holy and secular spaces. They can be thought of as a kind of transmitter between the two spheres. Through the doorway of the icon, the believer returns to the time and the place of the saints. The librarian's stare, the stare of the old tintypes, and the staring faces of *American Gothic* suggested the same kind of mirror or window. A way back to a time of communion and community. The citizens of Toledo were able to pick out their houses in the paintings of El Greco. Perhaps what sends me restlessly along these abandoned corridors in Iowa is the wistful notion that any place here can be that settled, settled enough to see itself as part of a continuing story. Part of a bigger picture.

. . . .

The signs are hand-painted and point to the *American Gothic* House or simply Gothic House. The route is also marked by the whitewashing of the curbing. I turned left into a neighborhood in the town's northeast corner. Then a right. Many of the houses share the carpenter Gothic frills and ornament—the endless porches, vertical siding, idiomatic outsized window. At first I felt I was missing something as I looked at the parade of houses, some now covered in asphalt shingling, some melting into Cape

Cod additions. Then it struck me. There were no foundations. The siding sprang right from the grass. The step up to the porches a board width at best. The large windows were level with my knees. I could step through them. Though they were old—the Gothic House is over one hundred years old—the little houses with half-stories felt temporary, as though they had been dragged there. Adding to this effect was the lack of shrubbery or flower beds. No foundation to screen. Only the buzzed brown lawn. At the end of the street, I took another left and crept past the town water treatment plant. A dusty, red pickup with a plastic tank in the bed was backed in to the building. The farmer was filling the tank, buying town water, while his kids ran ahead of me around the bend to the left to play in the cage of Eldon's tennis court. Wells were running dry that summer. The kids would exhaust themselves soon but find no shade in the broiling field where I parked.

Across the street the *American Gothic* House looked like its portrait. In the bright sun even the shadows, cut beneath the porch roof and cast by the lip of the famous windowsill, seemed generated by technique, the siding stained a permanent dark gray hue. The potted plants by the door were gone. A plaque commemorating the fiftieth anniversary of the painting and of the house being placed on the National Historic Registry was now attached to the front wall. The chimney had been capped, but that wasn't in the picture so it was hard to tell what was authentic. On the flat, brown lawn, halfway to the quiet, white house, two headless cutout figures cast long shadows up to the porch. The palette used to paint them was too bright; no attempt had been made to shade the wrinkles in the overalls. The perspective was about right, though placing the figures in the road itself would have been closer still to the exact dimension. The heads had been removed at the collars, the elongated style of the original helping the amputation. The bodies were to the proper human scale. Below the waists the artist was on his own and it showed. The hemline was wrong, and the shoes were too big and splayed out. I couldn't imagine actually having a picture taken this way although the graceful yoke of the collars beckoned. The house had a power in its whiteness, its stark cleanness of line. That power radiated. The whole lot was empty, cleared except for the cutouts. I wouldn't have been able to cross the road and step onto the property even if I had been with someone to take my picture in the pillory of the scene.

People still lived in the house. Wood told his sister, Nan, as she modeled the part of the spinster daughter, that he wanted to show the kind of people he thought lived there. He didn't want to disturb the real residents. Turns out Gideon and Mary Jones, grandparents to the owner of the Jones Cafe, lived in the house when Wood sketched it. Today the Hayneses, Kelly and Kelly, their two kids, her mother, and a niece live in the house surviving on welfare and disability checks. The rent is $50.00 a month, paid to Carl Smith of Cleveland who owns the place. When he dies, the house will be bequeathed to the state. The figures on the lawn were a compromise struck between the Hayneses and the people of Eldon who want to turn the house into a tourist attraction. The few tourists who find their way here can snap the pictures but the cutouts serve as scarecrows too. There were no tours of the house itself, but the space of the front lawn, the rendered public domain of the picture, no longer survives as private property. So this arrangement is part and parcel of the uneasy peace in this neighborhood, a tussle over borders and the waiting for a man in Cleveland to die. Everything shimmered the afternoon I stood and looked at the house. The light was almost Mediterranean. The heat made me sleepy. The house seemed to pulsate, dropped from the heavens on a freshly cleared landing zone. Staring at the house from across the road, I thought it too might be as flat as the headless figures propped in front of it. The electric blue sky became a matte, edging the iconographic outline of the house. If I looked hard enough I would be able to see through the window, see the depthlessness of the structure, see the sky on the other side.

It is a curious business, this seeing. So many small towns in Iowa seeking to diversify have fixed upon the idea of having people come see. The state estimates the cost of turning this house into a sight at $500,000, what with the renovations inside the house, the gift shop barn, the landscaping around the sludge lagoon, and the relocation of the Hayneses. A lot of people will have to find their way to Eldon and pay to look at the house before the town recovers the investment and then receives new income equal to the lost railroad payroll, the vanishing farm money. But still the scheme that will bring money in persists. The Jones Cafe, the only restaurant in town, acts as the locus of the tourist dream. There too you can buy the postcards and prints of *Stone City* and *The Birth Place of Herbert Hoover* by Wood and of a painting by Lee Allen, one of Wood's students.

The Window: The House 57 Years Later is a picture about looking. In the WPA style, Allen pays homage to his teacher. The house has been rotated slightly. We see it over the shoulder of another couple, an older man and woman dressed simply. The man is taking a picture of the house. The woman is looking at a picture of *American Gothic*, just about to look up and away from it to the house, judging the fidelity of the painting to the house and the house to the painting as we are judging the likeness she is holding to the original in our minds. To the right, a young boy straddles his archetypal cantilever bicycle—one foot on a pedal, the other on the ground—ducks his head, looks between the couple and the house, catching both in his peripheral vision. He can even see, out of the corner of his eye, the point of view of the painter, of the viewers. We take in the intense couple, the boy on the bike, and the two racing boys tearing up the road looking only at each other, gauging who is winning.

I am attracted to the timelessness of the scene, and I understand how compelling a timeless place can be. There are few of the precious places where things haven't changed, fewer still that have been doubly blessed, recorded by art's certifying glance. I remember coming upon the Sanitary Bakery on Bleecker Street in New York, amazed it survived pretty much unchanged from the Berenice Abbott photograph from the thirties. I knew the picture before the place. Now I was in the picture. It was almost as if taking the picture a half-century before had frozen the place itself, an image now of the image.

People will come to see the house in Eldon. It is something to see. Staking a whole economy around seeing it is another matter. The rewards of seeing this house are subtle and complex. Here public and private spaces meet; art meets life. The fact that someone still lives in the house makes the experience of seeing it richer. As an attraction, it would be a shell of what it was—a western stage set or a house in Henry Ford's Greenfield Village, where the man who invented the technology that destroyed the small town collected examples of houses. The Gothic House, as it is now, feeds the painting that made it famous. The painting's controlled statement of well-groomed household and modest prosperity is a pentimento ironically overlaying the contemporary hard-scrabble life of the Hayneses. The painting has always been misread, misread by Iowans, farmers, townspeople mistaking what the painting said to others about them. The painting has always been cursed and adored. What we see would be changed if the house became only a tourist stop. The rich confusion of art and life will be lost.

In its place what the house would become—a mock house, a cargo cult mock-up of a house luring in the tourist—will show through. The reasons to see the house will disappear once its only reason for being is to be seen.

When you drive the winding route to the Gothic House, look at the other houses along the streets. You will notice the ostentatious ornament of those houses, the windows, porches, and doors, as if each house were vying for the attention of an artist's eye, begging you to consider imagining the life led behind the façade. Even in this depression, in the obvious signs of hard times, the houses should claim your attention along with the scheming inhabitants behind the windows. And on the way out of town you must let your eyes follow that blasted corridor of an abandoned connection and begin to see the layers of meaning in the landscape and entertain the necessity of living ruins in your life.

LIVING DOWNTOWN

After ten years of living away from home, I took some time off from my job in Iowa to write a novel. I had most of a year, and I could have gone any place in the world. At the time I thought it was important to come back to Fort Wayne since that was where the novel was to be set and where my family still lived. So on a rainy fall day, I moved some books and papers and a suitcase of clothes into a furnished efficiency apartment in the Poagston Arms on Berry Street downtown.

The Poagston is one of the few tower apartment houses built in Fort Wayne. Unlike the new Three Rivers condominiums, the Poagston, built just after the Second World War, was never meant to be a luxury address. I suppose it had its big-city pretensions at the beginning with its green awning shading the entryway, streamlined brickwork and window treatment. It still retained the boom feeling of the war years when smart young women and working couples used to their independence and change in their pockets demanded a convenient address, efficient appliances, and minimal housekeeping. When it was built, perhaps everyone assumed that things would be growing downtown, that the Poagston was the first of many high-rises, a model for the city's future when Berry Street would be transformed into a scaled-down version of Park Avenue.

That's not the way things turned out, of course. When I moved in years later, the ten-story Poagston stood alone on its corner. The rest of the block had been cleared for parking lots used by the church across the street and another lot the Cadillac dealership wanted to abandon in a move out to the bypass. Berry Street was dotted with doctors' offices, more churches, a senior citizen center and housing complex, each with its own buffering parking lot, alternating to the center of downtown. I could live in the Poagston because it was cheap and there were several vacancies. It would be quiet. People, after all, hadn't wanted to live downtown. The future found people living in ground-hugging townhouses, a curious name, considering that they were arranged in cul-de-sacs, satellites, beyond the bypass highways that no longer bypassed a thing, so far from town. The bright young women were still there, my neighbors now, teachers mainly, nurses and legal secretaries who never married, close to retirement. They waited for the mail in the lobby as I moved in. They hadn't moved when the working couples had taken off to the suburbs when they were built. Strangely, it was not so much that the Poagston's time had come and gone; it always felt to me that the building's time had never come at all. It was like moving into someone's dream.

I never wrote that novel. The story was set during Prohibition and the Great Depression at the Irene Byron Tuberculosis Sanitarium outside of Fort Wayne. Another advantage of living downtown at the Poagston, I had thought, was the senior center down the street. I imagined I could go in during the day when the men were woodworking or shooting pool and the women were quilting or playing euchre and, with an introduction from my grandfather, start people talking about the times of the novel. I was especially interested in the downtown then, the way it stayed open all night, the lights of the dance halls and theaters, the sparks off the trolley wires, the spotlights on the mannequins in the windows of all the clothing stores. I wanted to imagine a downtown pieced together from stories my grandfather remembered or what I could coax from my parents: the press of all those people who were downtown for all kinds of reasons, not just to work at the banks and courthouse but to shop, to hang out and to meet up and to change buses and street cars, to transfer from home to work, the whole city circulating through its heart each day. I wanted to sense a kind of ambient noise for the background of my book. But those things had faded from my informants' memories, which had become as deserted as the downtown had. Instead they recalled more personal moments, the ambiguous feelings of how hard it was but how happy. Mainly we sat around the big table shaking our heads at the prices of things, then each trying to top the last—the number of hotdogs for a quarter, the distance traveled on a dime, the pounds of candy for a penny.

This failure in my research method didn't doom the novel. There were many things wrong with the idea, and I needed to write a bit of it to discover that. More interesting to me now was my original motivation to live downtown in the first place. Then, I believed it might help to write about Fort Wayne while living in it. What I discovered, of course, is that the city I wanted to write about, the one I had been writing about for ten years, was not the city I looked at day after day from my fifth-floor window in the Poagston. After a while I stopped working on the novel, started again on some stories about my Fort Wayne. But I also lived downtown in this other Fort Wayne, and part of the time, the part I wasn't dreaming, I walked the streets of the real city, which seemed ghostly compared to what I knew had been once. And it was pale shadow of what I was dreaming.

The window looked west. In the distance, the red flashing lights of the television towers pulsed after the sunset. I counted seven towers, their lights all on unique sequences. I had no television, only a radio that tuned in WOWO, but the flashing lights seemed to have a patient binary intelligence, messages written in the air. A block away was St. Joe Hospital where I had been born. It was close enough to see through the windows of the eastern façade into the rooms where the blue televisions seemed to float near the ceilings. I couldn't see the faces on the screens or the faces of the patients and nurses who moved from room to room. Below me on the other side of Fulton Street was the newspaper building parking lot that once had been Ed Harz's Standard Station, where my grandfather had moonlighted as an attendant all the time I was growing up. Then, at about this time of night, the nurses turned out the lights in the rooms, Ray tossed pizzas in his parlor next door (now also gone), and the *Journal* reporters filtered out of Henry's and crossed the street to work until deadline. That was about the time I'd come with my folks to pick up my grandfather from the station. He'd read the pumps and shut them off while we waited in the car. The lights went out. The twirling Standard sign stopped. Grandfather rattled the doors to make sure they were locked, then got in the car still smelling of gasoline and rubber. On some of those nights, my parents would tease him about Betty, who lived at the Poagston. Betty liked to come over to sit inside the station and talk to my grandfather between customers. She would leave as grandfather locked up, waving to us in the car, then walk back across the street.

When I lived in the Poagston years later, Betty was still there.

She introduced me around in the lobby while we were waiting for the mail carrier to finish sorting. "This is Jimmy's boy," she announced, never remembering she was skipping a generation. Other people used the lobby. There were offices on the ground floor and a music store, never open when I was around, its display window filled with huge brass tubas and sousaphones. When I turned eighteen, I had come down to the Poagston to the Selective Service office that had been here then to register. During the draft, the bus left at night from Fulton Street with the new inductees. Grandfather let them make collect calls those nights on the station phone. Selective Service wasn't there anymore, the draft now long gone. Vietnam veterans still came in looking for their organization's new office. The women in the lobby of the Poagston pointed them in the right direction. The veterans' new office around the corner on Berry was always filled, like the lobby of the apartment house, with people waiting. Most strange were the brain doctor's patients. Their heads were bandaged elaborately or were asymmetrically shaved, mapped with flaps and sutures. They too were a bit distracted. I am probably remembering selectively now. The lobby of the Poagston couldn't always have been populated by these brooding, staring people. I was one of them, I admit, turned inward by writing every day and by worrying my own past as it cycled through my fiction. I remember it raining all the time. That can't be true. But the ceiling above Fort Wayne is often low and gray, the roof of clouds bearing down from the Great Lakes. Leaving the building on those days, I stepped out on Berry where often it rained ashes. They were burning trash in the Poagston's incinerator.

My parents thought my living downtown in the Poagston was crazy. If I had moved home to write, why not move all the way home? I reminded them that they had sold my bed years ago. The message had been clear enough then. We all knew that if I was going to work I couldn't actually live at home. Their house elicited only holiday behavior. Christmas could not go on that long. Still, they felt they should say again that nobody lived downtown anymore.

They were partially correct. The old houses around the Poagston on the near west side of downtown had been cut up into doctors' suites or torn down for parking. A few of them had apartments for students at the art school or other young single people back from college who didn't want to move back in with their parents. There was some gentrification of the mansions and carriage houses, but it was half-hearted. One day I watched them move a three-story Victorian down Wayne Street in order to preserve it when the hospital needed more parking. It was to be used for doctors' offices. This neighborhood was mostly white. Then nearer in to downtown was the senior citizen housing project. On the east side was a black neighborhood of single family houses. I moved around south away from the river toward the old Central High School, closed now. The students who lived in its district were bused to the six high schools on the radiating outskirts of the city. People lived downtown. To my parents, to most of the city, it was just difficult for them to see this anymore. The people who lived downtown had become another type of ghost. Black families, the young and the old, single men and women. Even Vietnamese refugees were billeted that winter in the old Central Catholic High School. It was hard to integrate those definitions of living into greater Fort Wayne's sense of community. The feeling was amplified because there were few reasons to come downtown if you did not live there. Few people from the sprawling city's suburbs did find their way there. So, to them, there was nobody home downtown.

When the cognitive maps of a region are blank, I imagine they fill with frightening drawings of dragons, roughing in the terra incognita. I was crossing Fairfield one day walking downtown. The lights had stopped traffic on the avenue, and as I walked in front of the cars, I heard the clicks of the door locks. How I must have looked to these people when they were forced to stop and see me.

I felt very safe downtown mainly because I saw hardly anyone there at night after the banks closed. They cleared out at five, afraid of the emptiness that grows on their fear. Walking down Berry, I could see the Fort Wayne Bank building. Most of the façade was sheathed in marble, but from my angle, I could see the rougher brickwork on the side that had been hidden by an old hotel. I had watched them blow up the Van Ormen Hotel in what is the stunning state of the art now—that series of explosions ripping down the sides of the building, the way the floors float for a second before the squaring of their accelerating collapse takes over, the steaming pile of bricks and twisted reinforcing rods. One reason to make the trip downtown now is to see them blow it to bits. Downtown Fort Wayne was empty when I lived there. Whole blocks of parking lots were created as business moved away. A logic drove the destruction: parking would bring the people back downtown. You can see the footsteps of the progress, the gap-toothed architecture in the skyline. And the bank tower, as part of their international style, needed plazas and parks for people, their numbers constantly dwindling. There were fires that left holes when no one would invest. Temporary lots went in as the block lay fallow, a little outhouse hut near the gate. At night all the huts were empty, the cash register drawers left open to show me there was nothing to steal. When I lived in the Poagston, the city was still destroying itself in order to save itself.

It got very cold after Thanksgiving, and toward Christmas pipes burst in the Poagston. Parts of the building had no heat. I could see my breath as I sat in my tiny Murphy kitchen and typed. The manager came around when I called after I could take no more. I remember he walked into the room, hugged himself, and said, "You know, in Europe this wouldn't be considered cold." It was cold in Indiana though. The frost in the window had little spy holes I melted with my fingers so I could look over to the hospital. I packed up to wait it out at my parents', where I could have an excuse for not finishing much work.

I now had to drive downtown for my walks at night. During the day, I could ride the buses still running along the ancient trolley routes, though the demographics of the city had shifted. Most of the other passengers I rode with were the clients of the State Training Hospital which is near my parents' house. We were all getting off at the old transfer corner across from Murphy's. Downtown, Calhoun Street, even during the morning and evening rush, had been rendered desolate by its conversion into a transit mall. The big green buses alone in the newly bricked street lumbered up and idled as the clients dispersed to the departing buses that would take them to their jobs. We all waited in front of the boarded up storefronts while the new buses collected. And then they were all gone, the street empty without buses. I still couldn't bring myself to walk down the middle of the mall, though all were encouraged to do so.

I haven't mentioned any villains behind the transformation of this cityscape into a kind of desert. The year I was born saw the signing of the Defense Highway Act and the opening of the first McDonald's and Disneyland. It is too easy to anthropomorphize the car so I won't call it a villain, even though the power of the machine to recast the world is overwhelming. The culture of the car was pretty much established by the time I was born. The complete transformation took a while longer. I remember shopping for school clothes at Pat's downtown. My mother's hat and white gloves. And there are images of movies, photos from an old *Look* magazine which featured Fort Wayne right after the war as "The Happiest Town in America." In those pictures, Calhoun Street is choked with people. On the streets of Fort Wayne years later, I walked among ruins that were hard to see. It must have been like this for the Europeans when history began again in the Middle Ages. Walking the streets of their own cities, they realized for the first time that the Roman Empire had been dead for a long time. We believe we are the same people in the Happiest City, but we are not. We are something else, something we cannot begin to see.

They found and renovated the electric Santa Claus that W&D's Department Store once displayed each Christmas on the side of the old store when it was still open. That Christmas I lived in the Poagston, they hung it again on the side of the Fort Wayne Bank building. It was spectacular. I had never seen it before. Three stories, thousands of colored light bulbs, the ones on the runners of the sleigh strobing. The whip cracked with light. Toys spilled from the pulsing bag. The display had been forgotten even when I was a child and my parents took me downtown to the new store to see the animated window displays. W&D's had been closed for years. Someone stumbled on Santa in a warehouse that was being torn down.

The parking lot below Santa was filled with cars, engines running, windshields smeared with the lights. I watched the people inside craning to see up from under their car roofs the brilliant galaxy of light. A throbbing advertisement for a long-gone store was now a pure delight. Divorced from a forgotten past, it lit the sky with magic.

That same night, horses and carriages appeared on the

streets. The lights of the Santa Claus gleamed in the varnish finish of the phaetons and coupes. Some people did get out of their cars finally and took rides down Calhoun Street, the horses clopping through the red lights. I asked one of the drivers wrapped in a rug when the rides had begun and why. She said that she thought the time had come.

"It's like New York," she said. "Other towns are starting to do this too."

"And what do people look at?" I asked.

"The lights, I guess," she said. She pointed at the twinkling lights the city had strung on the new saplings planted along the transit mall.

. . . .

A few months later, I moved out of the Poagston Arms. I said good-bye to my friends in the lobby. Time is always an unseen component of a place. I sliced through this one moment of Fort Wayne. I took the train back out to Iowa. When I got there, it was night and it was spring.

FLYOVER

How did I know it was finally spring? This was in May, in Ames, Iowa. I was teaching at the university there. Between the administration building and the agriculture hall, in the middle of the campus, there is a ten-acre field that once had been a sheep meadow when the college was simply the state experimental farm. That meadow is now landscaped with all the trees and bushes indigenous to the state. I had heard that Frederick Law Olmsted, the architect of Central Park, had designed the plantings, but I could never prove it, such claims for his work were as common as the beds Washington slept in. In any case, the central campus was gorgeous, the flowering crab apples and dogwoods set against the oaks and freshening conifers with clumps of crocuses blooming at their feet. The grass looked painted green, the sun high enough in the sky at last to swab a shadow of the campanile, in a darker green, across it. Students lounged on the lawn using their books as pillows.

Still, these signs alone were not enough to convince me of the turn of the season. Having lived there only a few years, I had witnessed late winter storms howling in a wind the natives say blows unbroken from the Rockies. The sign I looked for was more superstitious, more magical. And there it was, the university's maintenance crews out on the lawn tearing down the snow fences, those pickets of cedar staves and twisted wire designed to knock down the wind's speed enough for the snow to drop out of the gale and drift away from the walkways. The snow fences, constructed in the fall, crisscrossed the campus. It always seemed to me they were like the decoy airplanes the cargo cults built on South Seas' islands. The fences worked better, however. They inevitably attracted the snow. Now that they were being rolled up, I could relax, stretch out and look up at that blue and endless sky above this part of the world.

The blue is so big you are convinced you can see the sky bend, shading in the periphery of your vision like the deep draping of silk. In Iowa, in the Midwest, you watch the sky a lot. You are drawn to its vastness, to your easy access to it, not just for the weather that actually delivers something to you and your neighborhood, but for the narrative the sky generates and transmits. You read it. Tune it in like another band of the radio waves it transports. The colors, the wind, the clouds pour over you scudding to the east, swimming upstream against the advancing sunlight. A film loop that never stops running from horizon to horizon, a ticker tape, a scroll.

There I was on that spring day once again reading the sky. Immediately, I saw in the air above Iowa the vapor trails of jets blooming behind the pinhead twinkle of the planes miles above me. On those days when the skies are cloudless, you can count ten or twelve flights streaking over, sketching out a corduroy weave to the sky. As one long arching cloud finally evaporated, two or three more were growing nearby, east to west, west to east. The planes crept back and forth, strangely mirroring the trajectory of tractors here on earth. They plowed the sky, turning over the blue field, leaving a furrow of jumbled and chunky clouds. The contrails hung there, it seemed, forever, and as they overlapped and smeared slightly in the prevailing wind, the sky, a cold clear glass, suddenly frosted with spiky fingers of water forming crystals.

As a midwesterner, I have thought, on those lazy afternoons looking up at the sky, what this place must look like from the air. Of course, I myself have been a passenger staring through the double-paned plastic window of a 737, noting the signature of the township grid, the rumpled patchwork quilt of the land. But most often I find myself as the observer stuck on the ground. This perspective suits me best, appropriate perhaps for one from this part of the planet. Perhaps as appropriate, I can't help projecting myself up to those planes. I adopt that point of view for the quarter hour the plane takes to stretch by overhead. Then I come back to earth.

I can't help but think of my earthbound state. After all, I know there are people riding by above me who consider this place, the Midwest, and the people who inhabit it "the Flyover," meaning to dismiss it, of course, as just an empty space that holds the two coasts apart. And those busy planes do seem like they are conducting important missions as they stride over us, inscribing their paths on the sky like those looping lines the airlines themselves draw on their route maps of the United States. "Look," those charts seem to say, "an easy hop, skip, and jump over all this blank space."

Sometimes, I believe this implied message that the busy air traffic of people going places graphically illustrates. But more often I think that those passengers above don't know what they are missing. With that in mind, I would wrap those lovely spring days around me, keeping what I know of this place a secret. Let altitude then be the best defense and let the midwesterner wear the mantle of "the Flyover" as a kind of camouflage. Down below I'll be waving, waving, glad to see those above rush by, taking with them those streaked mental snapshots they've recorded from their cramped coach seats as souvenirs of the Midwest and their few minutes above us.

The truth is that such an ambiguous feeling about the Midwest seems to me to be very midwestern. Simultaneously, a midwesterner can imagine himself mired at the end of the earth and ensconced at its very heart. The conflict between the ideals of community and mobility has long been a central drama of America itself, but only in the Midwest, it seems to me, is this drama expressed so subtly and engrossingly. If the rest of Americans knows anything about this region they know it as the place where something or someone is *from*. Midwesterners themselves have a harder time simply saying where this place is.

For this essay the states of Ohio, Indiana, Michigan, Wisconsin, Minnesota, North Dakota, South Dakota, Nebraska, Kansas, Missouri, Illinois, and Iowa will make up our flyover. My students in Iowa always excluded Ohio and Michigan from their maps of the Midwest as eastern states. Growing up in Indiana, I would never include Missouri, too southern, or Kansas, too western, in my cognitive setup. I bet if you ask a resident of any of our target states they would affirm without question that the ground they are standing on is pure midwestern soil. They might go on then and amend the appellation, Midwest, with "Upper" or "eastern" to fit in those other states. Or ask them for the region's identifying characteristics. You will probably get a description of a "typical" midwestern state that matches the habitat of your informant's. The Midwest is farming and small towns if you are from Iowa, not just any old farming but corn farming. From Indiana, I always thought a mixture of medium-sized industrial cities and small farms were needed as the ingredients of any midwestern composition. That's the rub. No one really knows where or what the Midwest is. We could argue all day about its geography, its demographics, heck, even its ethos. My definition, finally, evolved to incorporate that basic mystery, the area's own invisibility to itself. No one knows for sure where it is, but everyone is sure it is great to be from there.

The Midwest, because it is so vast and diverse, is largely invisible, not only to those rushing through it or over it, but even to those who live within its borders. It is hidden in plain sight. Often, those of us who live here have grown used to the subtle and varied pleasures of this home and have come to think of where we live as a basal line of experience from which the extremes of other regions spike above and below our expectations. For bicoastal travelers, this notion adds a discriminating lens to their bird's-eye view. But for midwesterners, this act of imagining an aerial angle provides a platform from which to observe ourselves and our surroundings, perhaps for the first time. It gives us just enough distance to picture ourselves without stepping out of the picture all together.

There are the old jokes, black-out sketches and cartoons, about the amateur photographer with a Brownie camera taking group pictures at a certifiably photogenic locale, the Grand Canyon, say, or Big Sur, Pikes Peak, or the Everglades, and, being so involved with the arrangement of the image in the viewfinder, he directs his subjects or himself off the nearby cliff or back into the swampy water. Imagine now such a setup in the Midwest. The photographer, chances are, could tell his whole extended family to take a step back for almost forever and, most times, never approach the lip of any danger.

The Midwest is hard to see especially when you are in it. In the photos we take of ourselves, we tend to think of the background of where we live as just that, background. Our families, our friends are most often our subjects. The background is seldom, if ever, a picture in its own right. It isn't one we keep. Those other pictures, those thrilling vistas, we believe are somewhere else. Perhaps that is why so many of us can't imagine missing that background until we've moved away or why I project myself up to the clouds to get some perspective. This hovering seems necessary, a way to build a mountain view into the plains and prairies, the still lakes and rolling hills we think we know like the backs of our hands.

. . . .

Living in a flat land, I have always wanted to be able to gaze down on the world. Chicago obliged. My earliest memories are of taking trips to Chicago, the birthplace of the skyscraper, and climbing to the observation decks of the tall buildings. First, there was the Standard Oil Building near the lake, where I thrilled each time a little airplane settled on Meigs field below. From up there, I imagined, you could see the lake shore curve all the way back to Indiana, and from there I also watched the cranes and construction workers stitch together the *X*s of the Prudential Building. And once that building was finished, from the platform there, do I remember looking down at the Standard Oil Building where I once stood? From the Prudential Building, I could see, close up, the fine detail of the Tribune Tower and the Wrigley Building and stare at the hypnotic rhythm of the Marina Towers, the Corn Cobs, near the river where, nearby, the asymmetrical shafts of black glass raced each other to the top of the Sears Tower. On that observation deck, every time I'm there, I call home from one of the pay phones. All of the towers have a radio station broadcasting from their peaks. As I'd talk with my folks, I could read the deejay's lips in his glass booth, both of us hoping our messages would convey our new take on the world. The sky, in my memory, always severely clear, opened up forever. Only the earth's gentle curve ever obstructed the view. From the angle of the observation deck you can make up a kind of sense of what's below. You want to share it with as many people as you can. Once I watched a fleet of helicopters lift off from Grant Park, a President and his entourage thundered by at eye level on the way to O'Hare. Up there, I could get closer than any parade route on the ground.

. . . .

As I thought about the Midwest as the Flyover, I found myself thinking about flight in general. Perhaps you wouldn't associate the Midwest with flying. After all, this region seems relentlessly earthbound. There is so much of it. Then again, what region could be more fertile in creating the daydreams of flight? I'm not the first midwesterner who has felt the tug of gravity and conjured up ways to escape it. As I said, we are of two minds or, better yet, two mediums, rooted down to earth and with our heads in the clouds. Many places in the Midwest are connected to the seemingly indifferent flight paths that arch above them. Let me map a constellation of aviation shrines. I'll do my own flyover of the territory, an acrobatic touch-and-go on the route our reconnaissance planes have taken.

Beginning in Ohio, we discover the Wright brothers themselves in their Dayton bike factory. There, now, is the Air Force Museum with its huge hangar-like building that is still not large enough to house the sparkling B-36. And up the road is Wapakoneta where Neil Armstrong was born. His own moon-shaped museum looks like it is in close synchronous orbit, floating a few feet above a green Ohio hillock. In Indiana, where the Wright brothers were born and Armstrong went to school,

Purdue University, the *alma mater* of astronauts, once owned Amelia Earhart's Lockheed Electra. She was still a member of the faculty when she disappeared over the Pacific. In Michigan, Ford built the famous Tri-Motor, and when he couldn't get the real thing for his museum in Greenfield, collected the replica of the *Spirit of St. Louis,* the one that Jimmy Stewart flies in the movie. Across Lake Michigan in Wisconsin, Oshkosh hosts its annual fly-in with its home-built craft that look like bicycles with wings the Wright brothers could have built. Experimental planes made out of laminated graphite, ancient biplanes, and GeeBees jam the summer sky. Vintage fighters and Piper Cubs circle in circus colors or camouflage. Further west in Minnesota, the birthplace of Lindberg himself, pontoon planes set down on remote lakes. Beneath the wheat fields and sunflowers of the Dakotas, the planted missiles in their silos that are supposed to never fly. In Omaha, SAC Headquarters hopes to become as sleepy as the hundreds of wind sock, grass runway airparks that dot the fields. Their big bombers once dipped down to the deck and practiced tree-top flying, skimming over the grassland and the sand hills. And then I think of Kansas and the factories in Wichita, the production lines of single-family Cessnas, executive jets, turbo-propped puddle jumpers for the growing commuter trade, and even the President's new customized jumbos parked wing-tip to wing-tip on broiling tarmac. Missouri has its own factories for high-performance military planes, and St. Louis, of course, gave its name to the most famous airplane in the world. At Ida Grove, in Iowa, each summer they refight the Battle of Britain with an armada of quarter-scale, radio-controlled model Spitfires and Stukas. How would this fly-in look from the air? Tiny airplanes zipping through the oily smoke of smudge pots set in burning cardboard cities. In Chicago, I also remember gazing up at the life-sized dogfight near the ceiling of the Science and Industry Museum where the real fighters and bombers hung frozen there in pitched battle and served as a model for my own homely dioramas suspended from the ceiling fixtures of my bedroom. There, I strung up plastic models of the *Spirit of St. Louis*, the DC-3, and the P-39, which was built in my hometown during the war. I had pieced them together from kits stamped out in still more factories not far from Chicago. There, too, O'Hare, the world's busiest airport, sits daily inhaling and exhaling the waves of its commercial traffic. Chances are the sophisticated air traveler who sniffs at the Flyover doesn't fly over it at all anymore but descends to one of the several hubs in Chicago, Detroit, Minneapolis, Kansas City, and St. Louis and connects with the remaining spoke of a flight.

. . . .

In Hitchcock's *North by Northwest*, the fleeing Cary Grant has been instructed to wait for a contact in the middle of an Indiana cornfield. A bus delivers Grant to the rendezvous site, and it is incredibly desolate, here and there a few stands of corn. Midwesterners know that this can't possibly be Indiana. The horizon is too far away, and the land is (and this is possibly) *too* flat. Hitchcock probably filmed it in a California desert, importing the stalks of corn. But the spirit of the place is right. What's on the screen is a massaged landscape that, at first glance, looks natural but on closer inspection yields evidence of complex human tinkering. That replicates the Midwest. It masquerades as wild while it is rich with human drama. There, in the sky, off in the distance we now see the tiny speck of the crop duster banking, dipping its nose down toward the clueless Grant. The setting of Indiana, of the Midwest, is a crucial part of this famous scene. There is a stark beauty in the minimal props of the still life and the dome of sky that arches over it. The landscape mirrors the frighteningly different world in which the protagonist has been plunged. It is so strange. It has something to do with scale. The sky in the Midwest is just big enough. Even in the most wide open of places in the Midwest there is still something, far off, bounding it. There are always limits to what you see. No place is completely empty. That copse of trees in the distance, that grassy ridge, that elevator or water tower, they are like islands in an ocean. They turn the space of the sea into a wide-open bay.

I have been thinking a lot about the sky and its relation to the Midwest. When I first moved to Iowa, back to the Midwest from graduate school in Baltimore, a friend from North Dakota gave me a huge poster published by the National Weather Service. It was a cloud chart designed as a spotter's guide with pictures of three dozen kinds of clouds, all named with biological-sounding Latin and labeled with an alphabet of iconographic symbols. There is *Altocumulus Translucidus Undulatus*, the buttermilk sky, or *Cirrus Uncinus*, the wisp of the mare's tail. My favorite was assigned the code M 9, a middle cloud of the ninth kind, called *Altocumulus of a Chaotic Sky*. Working in my office, I'd take a break occasionally and gaze out the window, sometimes using a pair of cheap binoculars, to focus on a passing cloud. I kept a log of my sightings in the way birders keep track of their species.

In the creative writing classes I taught, my students would write that their stories and poems were taking place beneath the Iowa sky, and I would criticize them for not being specific. "What is an Iowa sky?" I'd ask. "What is Iowa, for that matter?" For them it was so obvious as to be forgotten. They assigned the name to the sky as a shortcut to communicate where they were. I knew the feeling. I too grew up in the Midwest never really thinking about it as a place of any distinction. My home state was just a name. But I had left for a bit and lived under other skies. Returning home, I needed such a chart to help me find where I was. After classes in which I tried to convince my students to sharpen their eyes, I'd rush back up to my own perch and sweep the air for clues. I wanted to see not only what heaven looks like but what that heaven looks down upon.

The Great Lakes

The author Donald Barthelme in his story, "Up, Aloft in the Air," imagines the science fiction comic book hero Buck Rogers having a typical pulp adventure in another unknown part of the galaxy, only in this version the galaxy is Ohio and the various "planets" he lands on are inhabited by the Tire Builders of Akron, the Glass Blowers of Toledo, The Coal Stokers of Cleveland. Buck, parachuting through the night sky, hurtles toward Cincinnati below. Listen, as he contemplates his future:

> "What is your life-style, Cincinnati?" Buck asked the recumbent jewel glittering below him like an old bucket of industrial diamonds. "Have you the boldness of Cleveland? the anguish of Akron? the torpor of Toledo? What is your posture, Cincinnati?" Frostily the silent city approached his feet.

It is a funny story because it toys with a truth of this part of the Midwest. The states that border the Great Lakes (Ohio, Michigan, Indiana, Wisconsin, Minnesota) are rich with cities and towns made famous for making something famous. Much of the landmass here was drained of the primordial swamp that feeds the lakes and yet this stretch of territory still can be thought of as a busy archipelago of city-states like the chain of towns of ancient Greece that ringed the Aegean and dotted its scattered islands. Each has its own character, autonomy, and history. I remember once flying over this region at night. From the high altitude of a coast-to-coast flight, I looked down to where the blacked-out lakes sliced their familiar shapes along the shores. There, the smear of lights of Milwaukee and Detroit. Off in the distance, I saw Cleveland, its northern rim surgically sculpted by the scoop of the darkened lake. Below me was my own hometown, Fort Wayne, beneath a layer of clouds, the lights of its cock-eyed grid showing through as if covered by a feathery mold. Beyond that I could distinguish Toledo too and Lansing, and then, smaller still, towns like Garret and Bowling Green and Coldwater. Each a distinct cluster of light connected only by a jeweled web of the thinnest gossamer threads. It did look like outer space, a chart of spinning individual galaxies.

Circleville, Ohio, is known for its pumpkins. Blue Earth, Minnesota, is known for the Jolly Green Giant. Wausau, Wisconsin, is known for its insurance. Warsaw, Indiana, is the world capital of artificial knees and replacement hips. In Bryan, the Ohio Art Company follows the ancient craft of constructing Etch-A-Sketches. Battle Creek builds cereals; Muncie builds mason jars; and Oshkosh builds jeans. In Auburn they built Auburns and Cords and Dusenbergs, the survivors of the species returning to the Indiana village each Labor Day like swallows to Capistrano. There are glass cities and seats of furniture. Homes of flags and birthplaces of cheeses. Lima gave its name to the best steam engines in the history of the world. There are towns famous for bikes, canal boats, lentils, Bing cherries, mint, jams, jellies, preserves, spark plugs, band instruments, copper wire, mobile homes, motorcycles, the Dum-Dum sucker, and even the kitchen sink. These towns are like diminutive solar systems; the life of each town orbits the bright center of its product, produce, or past, its identity caught up in the gravity of the plant or the plant. Even the larger cities participate in this reduction to a simple common denominator, the brewers of Milwaukee for example. And what do they do in Detroit?

The chambers of commerce and the Main Street boosters of these towns and cities work hard to construct a unique identity for each place. And though the larger cities sprawl, you still can feel that there is some space between such urban growth. Town and country can be defined. The landscape is still pieced together like a quilt, the fabrics forming an interesting texture emerging from the juxtaposition of rural and urban. That is not to say that this stretch of land is only a random and scattered assortment of summer festivals and museum displays. The states of the Great Lakes are knit up in several rich dense networks of roads and waterways, trails and trunk lines, rails and right-of-ways. The peculiar geological formation of the Great Lakes, the great big footprint of the last glacier, has squeezed and channeled the means of egress west. The Lakes funnel the turnpikes and the interstates along what the old Railroad PR called the water level route. That western expansion barreling through here is the most obvious migration in our past, but, for the Midwest, the migration from south to north was just as shaping though more subtle. What remains is the residue of macadam, cement, steel, and tar. It is the physical warp and woof of the comings and goings through this region. The roads truly crossed here and still do.

People and goods have always moved through in all directions, and those that settled participated in the rounds of the tight weave of their own regional business. So it seems appropriate that so much of the energy and industry expended here goes toward making things that move. Cars, of course, and all the parts that go into them, and trains (Amtrak still shops its cars in Indianapolis), but also wagons, for both the farm and the playground, tractors and bikes both human and motor powered. Even ships.

We tend to think of the Midwest as landlocked, but the Lakes, even before the Seaway was opened, teemed with ships plying the waters. After all, isn't it funny, we call them lakes. To call them lakes is to make this inland sea diminutive and manageable. Each basin gets assigned its own quirky character like those distinguishing characteristics we assigned to the small towns. The Lakes are our Mediterranean, the water around the center of our world. Through this waterway the Atlantic has always been connected to the Gulf of Mexico, first by portages, then by canals, followed by the railroads and the highways. I watched once from a high-rise apartment in downtown Detroit the parade of ocean-going ships soon after ice-out, the lakes turning liquid again in the spring. As I called out the colors and designs painted on the passing ships' funnels, my host named the heralds of companies from everywhere on earth. The landing craft for D-Day were built in Evansville, Indiana, and floated down the Ohio River. This region was once a swamp, and a wetland might serve as an appropriate metaphor for what it still is. Things percolate constantly through this place. The region is spongy with its own mobility, but resilient in its steeping. It seems to float and stay put.

Remember that these states were the first colonies of the United States. This region was systematically settled under a plan informed by the ideals of the American Revolution and the Enlightenment philosophers that sparked it. Perhaps that is why it is so easy for us still to picture so many places as if they were strange new planets. They were founded as the imaginary outposts, experiments in civics projected by the fledgling institutions of an invented and idealistic nation. These towns reflect the desire to create a rational, classical civilization in the wilderness. O brave new world!

These towns are not simply similes of the city-states of the golden age. You must think of them also as actual studied replicas of that model. You find the pillars and Parthenons of ancient Greece embodied again in the dozens of small colleges and universities spread throughout the region. Most claim the title "Athens of the Midwest." Start with Athens, Ohio, itself, the site of Ohio University. Are we Buck Rogers on this trip or Thucydides? Visit the New Critics of Kenyon, the Musicians of Oberlin, Antioch with its colonies, Denison perched upon its acropolis, the Gentlemen of Wabash, the Scholars of Depauw, the Hillsdale Economists, the Ripon Debaters, Carlton Writers, and St. Olaf, the home of the brave. The quads of the colleges mapped out on their wooded hills float above the shaded streets of their various sees. Perhaps they represent a more sublime manufactory of local enterprise, but the colleges partake of the same dream of the Midwest. These schools, with their infinite variations, also express that desire to build something, to grow something, to make something go.

What with all this talk of civilization one would think that the shade of the old forests had been crosshatched off the map by the intersecting lace of highways. It exists still on the fringes of the region. The wooded bluffs of the Ohio River valley, the tangled karst of southern Indiana and the green kettles of Wisconsin, the worn wilderness of the northern peninsulas and the swampy scrub of the boundary waters. In these places the busy civic tinkering never quite took. In many of the deserted spots, the growth, though aging, is new. Often this is second- or third-growth forest and those hills are reclaimed. The new vegetation obscures our own sets of ruins, another parallel with the ancient world. I am thinking of the played-out limestone quarries near Bedford and Oolitic, whose tumbled blocks could be the remains of an amphitheater near Mount Pelion. Or the strip mines around Zanesville or the leveled iron mountains of the Mesabi Range. Or even the pit in my hometown, the deepest hole in Indiana, out of which we hauled sand and stone to make the roads. These holes are strangely beautiful and sad now the way all ruins are. They are the ultimate monuments to our industry. In their depth they express the negative space of our capability. I always thought that the Empire Quarry should look like an exact mold from which the complete chiseled shaft of the Empire State Building was extracted. The holes that dot this region demonstrate clearly the law of conservation of matter. Here we have a clear record of what remains and what has gotten up and gone.

. . . .

Harvey Pekar is a hospital file clerk in Cleveland. He is also the author of a comic book series called *American Splendor.* His stories reverse the assumptions Donald Barthelme makes in "Up, Aloft in the Air." Pekar, a native, doesn't see Ohio as a strange new universe. He writes relentlessly about ordinary life in his city—a journey to the corner deli, the search for a friend up at the airport, the adventure of finding a stamp. But these stories, drawn beautifully by a wide variety of comic book artists (R. Crumb, Drew Friedman, Zabel and Dumm, to name a few), appear in a form, the comic book, usually reserved for the likes of superheroes and masked crime fighters. The effect is quite stunning. *American Splendor* captures the subtle splendor of this neck of the woods. We watch as daily life reveals itself in the setting of grand and sweeping epic.

The Great Plains

In Glenn Meeter's story "A Harvest," the narrator, an eastern office worker, drives with his farmer brother-in-law, Gerard, down the middle of the Great Plains, north to south on US 281, against the ripening tide of the wheat harvest. It is a breathless, contemplative story of long sentences that mimic the endless road, a story about many things, about our transformation from a rural to an urban race, about the kinds of intelligence with which such places and professions endow us. The story is also about life being a journey and about history existing in the present moment:

> Your point is the whole ecology of the plains is a web of civilizations weaving—cattle from Scotland, and England and Holland, the horse from Spain, the Chinese elm, the Russian olive, the exotic pheasant, the wheat itself, all from Asia, hardly one thing unimported in all the rustic prairie. . . . Greeley, Nebraska, a town with shaggy elms and sewers that hump the road, was named for a journalist who was himself named Horace after the Roman poet. . . . Outside the narrow sun-drenched streets of St. Paul, Gerard jabs a finger: "There's wheat." It is his language, *his* harsh vowels and blurred consonants, that has power. *Thairzweet.* There's wheat, there's wheat; Garden City has froze out, but here by God there's wheat! Green waves break past the window into individual spears, drilled in rows. There's wheat.

By the end of the story, Meeter's city-dwelling protagonist has made his peace with the alienating openness of the Great Plains by stringing the sensations of his 700-mile trip together into one long satisfying narrative:

> Drowsy, the mind blinks: pheasant in horizontal flight, yellow-bibbed lark, fiery wheat, heavy harvesters, red dirt and white dust, sunlight's stab on glass, gravel oil, wide Slavic forehead, Grainbelt, Champlin, Allis-Chalmers, and aloft with the merest forward effort, a hawk . . . yes you would do it again, touching nothing, learning nothing, doing nothing at all, but my God what a delight, just to travel through.

The distribution pattern of cities and towns around the Great Lakes implied a model of city states, of ancient Greece or Renaissance northern Italy. On the Great Plains of North and South Dakota, Nebraska, and Kansas the feeling is almost Roman in its vastness and in the way its inhabitants administer space. The township squares are bundled up into larger and larger units of measure. Here, people speak of whole mile-square sections as if they were acres. The space is not so filled up by the habitats of the inhabitants as is true further east. Here, we like to say, there is plenty of parking. But the presence of human intervention is everywhere, as Meeter suggests above, a web of civilizations weaving.

Center-pivot irrigation rigs, all struts and frets, wire and tubing, stride around their endless courses. Huge radar arrays that look like wire-mesh pyramids picket the border with Canada. You get a sense of the cybernetic workings of the reservoirs and channels all along the Missouri River watershed, of sluices opening and closing and lakes filling and emptying on their own, responding to an elaborate array of sensors and weather feedback. Trains, hundreds of covered grain hoppers long, painted the pastel colors of after-dinner mints, are piloted by crews of merely two. Strings of black coal gondolas stream from the pits of the Powder River to the power plants of the Great

Lakes. There are no more cabooses, those rolling houses. Instead, spliced between the freight cars are burbling helper engines, linked by remote with the pilot diesel out in the lead. The traffic on all of the tracks is controlled by radio and computer from the main offices as far away as Omaha or the suburbs of Chicago. These public and private works are Roman in feel and sometimes even look like the aqueducts or fortifications or roadbeds of that empire that our engineers and architects studied in school and replicated here. At times, our modern talent for automating creates the strange sensation that these massive machines run on their own as if their builders were part of an ancient and now extinct culture, their programs still running in the guts of their creations, shunting raw materials, energy, and water around the plain.

Monumental construction is not always utilitarian. Often the monuments are as likely to be patriotic expressions of power and grandeur as follies of playful dreamers. The pouting heads of Mount Rushmore seem to out-Roman the Romans in memorializing. The mountain is neighbored now by the equally impressive carving of Crazy Horse. There is the Corn Palace with its exfoliating seasonal façade, its onion domes sometimes sporting a thin metallic leaf of onion seeds or golden sunflower petals, its pediment commemorating bumper crops instead of the defeat of the Gauls. Along I-80, the rest stops exhibit out-sized sculpture in a lineal art museum that stretches across the whole state while advertisements of Wall Drugs radiate from its source on the plain. Back in Nebraska, a replica of Stonehenge, the monoliths replaced by the crushed bodies of cars, is perhaps the most ambitious of the playful monuments that dot the prairie. A three-story bison here, here a twenty-foot-tall prairie chicken, here a house-sized snapping turtle made from iron wheel rims, here a ball of string so huge it must be housed under the roof of its own gazebo in a city park, and here a city park landscaped around the salvaged gun turrets and superstructure of a moth-balled battleship. All of these edifices stand out in contrast to the broad sweep of canvas the landscape provides. The broadness and flatness of that canvas, perhaps, is the inspiration for the scale of such gigantic undertakings. The land itself gets in the act, creating its own monuments. The geography contains pockets of geological oddities, unique and obvious sacred precincts. The Badlands, the Sand Hills, the Flint Hills, the Black Hills, and the Loess Bluffs all created by the ever present wind itself, sculpting its own alluvial gesture with its scouring hand on the plain.

. . . .

In 1977, a Kansan, Elizabeth Layton, began to produce pictures of herself using a method called contour drawing, which asks the artist to copy, without looking down at the paper, the contours of the subject. "Grandma" Layton was sixty-eight when she began to draw her remarkable self-portraits using thirty-five-cent white poster paper and colored pencils purchased from the Wellsville drugstore. Her work has been compared to Chagall for its magical intensity and the buoyant, graceful weightlessness. Her figures vibrate and flow like those of Thomas Hart Benton. The renderings of herself are brutally honest. In one, *Intensive Care Room, 1978,* she places herself beside her adult son's deathbed, the contours of her face screwed together in anguish. Balancing on the tip of his pictured finger Layton has affixed a Red Cross blood donors pin, a drop of bright red. What strikes you is the line you are following on the paper, its wavy thinness dividing the huge white spaces into quivering and quite moving shapes.

You cannot help but think of lines and the contours they trace when you think of this region. The line expresses itself minutely in the quivering hand of a native or grandly with a combine cutting a swath through the wheat. Somewhere out there is the line between dry land ranching and farming. You'll know you've crossed it if, on one summer night, you find while driving east that suddenly your pristine windshield is studded with the remains of hundreds of smashed bugs. Out there also is the hundredth meridian, to some the cultural and psychic continental divide of the continent. Or follow the contour suggested by the geometric vector angling from the geographical center of the continental United States outside Lebanon, Kansas, and the geographical center of the United States near the Belle Fourche Reservoir of South Dakota. Or think of President Franklin Roosevelt dreaming, those Dust Bowl summers, of creating his own monument, a shelter belt of trees that would gird this waist of the nation with a wall of trees. You see that dream survive in the living dotted lines of windbreaks forming groves around the surviving homesteads, the five rank plantings of cedar, Russian olive, and cottonwood.

Vertical lines have always been the most striking here. Trees, windmills, grain elevators, church spires. Their stark perpendicular contrast graphically captures the stark and beautiful image of this place. The vertical line when it arranges itself into something like a silver water tower floating over a town breaks the monotony and the power of the horizon. These ordinary structures become monument, more markers on the plain. Sullivan and Wright quote this startling contrast in the design of their skyscrapers and prairie bungalows, the horizon launching the spire. But out here on the Great Plains, we look for anything, a fence post or a person standing up in the high prairie grass, that will lead the eye up from the flat earth to the paralleling flat sky.

The Great River

In the fragment, "Crossing the Mississippi," Ernest Hemingway writes of the ordinariness of the river as his hero, Nick Adams, sees it for the first time:

> Nick had expected bluffs for the Mississippi shore but finally, after an endless bayou had poured past the window, he could see out the window the engine of the train curving out onto a long bridge above a broad, muddy brown stretch of water. . . . Anyhow I've seen the Mississippi, he thought happily to himself.

What does make the Mississippi the Mississippi? And why does it occupy such a mythic niche in our imaginations? "The Great Brown God," the Missourian T. S. Eliot called it from the distance of Europe. Here I am, with this brief essay, beginning to add to the total wordage expended on the thing, on the brink of adding my own rhapsodic epithet to the pile. After all, Nick's initial perception is accurate. There is not much particularly to comment upon. We don't hold dear the Mississippi for its raw power or its unique beauty. The hazy rainbow refracted in the falls at Niagara or the flashing fish ladders of the Columbia make better postcards. Even the river's title as "Father of Waters" is not quite right since the Mississippi doesn't spawn tributaries as much as it drinks them in, a braid of rivers. Still, the Mississippi generates legend in the way other streams generate voltage. The surprise always is that once you see it, you ask yourself what all the fuss is about. My point, I guess, is that meaning is never inherently present. It gets attached to the river by the formulation of the stories we tell about it, and those stories, like the allusions to Huck and Tom suspended in Nick Adams's stream of consciousness, begin to accumulate and build a fine silt.

Illinois, Iowa, and Missouri make up the delta of the river's ability to contribute stories to our collective unconscious. They share in a kind of Doppler effect. When we try to focus on these states as a subject, layers of other meanings attach freely to their landscapes. Soon, stories about a place are in the foreground and obscuring the ground itself. Robert Frost said that a poem must mean at least one thing and at least one thing more. These states are like poems because they not only possess unadorned ordinariness but its very abundance makes our jump to the hyperspace of metaphor and myth an easy step.

Here are some examples. In Chicago's Art Institute, civic pride has conserved the old trading floor of the Chicago Board. In other parts of town, real men and women in real, bright-colored jackets continue to gesticulate and shout their puts and calls in the commodities pits. But in the museum the floor is quiet, and you can marvel at the gas lamps and the old stained wood. Back in one corner, on a table there are small piles of oats, corn, wheat, beans, and barley. The sign tells you that these samples served to remind the traders of just what they were trading in the pits (the pits already the symbolic residue of the actual trading pit where farmers once dumped their grain at market). Now, even that thin tether has snapped, and the trading floors operate today in a realm of their own abstraction. You can watch the action from the galleries, looking down on the real floors as if you are appreciating another art form, a kind of dance or theater performance.

Elsewhere whole towns participate in the same kind of myth-making. Communities brush up daily against the fuzzy membrane that separates reality from the stories we make up about it. In Galena, Illinois, the populace conspires to keep the village one hundred years behind our time. Its industry is antiques and the consumption of the picturesque. Downriver,

Branson, Missouri, has become the city fueled by country music. There, individual singing stars construct their own elaborate compounds to spin their stories of a made-up common past. In the suburban hamlet of Urbandale, Iowa, Living History Farms operates several working spreads arranged to simulate various strata of time, including the future. Visitors drift from one era to the next. And out on the river itself, paddleboats now ply the water again, re-creating the gambling past, though the stakes are lower. Meanwhile inland, streamlined dinner trains steam nightly, going nowhere, trundling back and forth across the storied prairie, echoing the elegance of first-class rail travel we've only seen in the movies. All across the region there are these bubbling springs that issue forth stories and images about ourselves.

The ability of this fertile valley to represent itself as typical, as ordinary, has spawned all manner of media to convey the message. In a country that is still inventing itself, the skill at creating a common and commonly held culture is quite remarkable. In Kansas City, Hallmark launches millions of brilliant scripts that allow the sender and the receiver to act out every nuance of a relationship. In Des Moines, the Meredith Company's *Better Homes and Gardens* appoints model living rooms with the furnishing of dreams; their test kitchens revise the American palette. The books they publish paper the walls of bookstores with possibilities. Even Chicago's professional sports teams participate in the general myth-making. In baseball, the sport known for its dexterity at meaning something more than a sport, there is no more storied team than the Cubs with their only recently illuminated field unless, of course, it is the Sox saying it ain't so.

Another, more recent, formulation of the White Sox story has the ghost of Shoeless Joe appear out of a cornfield onto a rough ball diamond a farmer has constructed on his land in Iowa. "Is this heaven?" he asks. "No," comes the reply, "It's Iowa." Iowans seriously considered stamping a message similar to this on their license plates. To say what? To tell the rest of the country of Iowa's own special election, its fortuitous combination of gifts. But more importantly, the bit of dialogue they'd carry around on their car bumpers was directed at themselves, at Iowans, who must daily flex the muscle of imagination, to see the potential in their surroundings, to cast themselves in an artistic and epic drama.

At the heart of this drama is the notion of the Heartland that midwesterners must wear upon their sleeves. We can't seem to forget we live daily near this magic spot. The emotional center of the country seems all around us. Earlier, I mentioned that the geographical centers of the United States and the continental United States were located out on the Great Plains. For a moment, I imagined some government-sponsored surveying team out on the prairie burdened by maps, photos from outer space, and the apparatus needed to plot the ground precisely. What a job! But you know it's true. Somebody did figure it out. Those centers are real enough. They can be measured and marked. But in this triangulation of emotion, the Heartland of America, there are no physical or mathematical formulas for affixing an X to the site. In this basin of the "Father of Waters," we feel we are close to it and feel the weight of knowing we are.

Does it play in Peoria? Is there a Little Old Lady from Dubuque? Walking these archetypal streets are our cultural icons. They live. I've been to Eldon, Iowa, where the carpenter Gothic house painted behind Grant Wood's severe couple in *American Gothic* still stands. In this light, it is difficult too to see Lincoln or Truman through the thick cloak of stories that adhere to their legends. Illinois's own license plate transforms the whole state to "the Land of Lincoln" after all. Truman's Independence stands for something else now as if the name of his town was imprinted on his genes.

It is the special burden of living here at the center of the country. The dendritic pattern of the Mississippi looks like the map of the nation's central nervous system. How easily this river and its tributaries come to stand for something else. The fault lines of the national character run through here also, and the natives of this place spend a lot of their free time mulling over the special circumstances of living so close to the emotional epicenter. There is a real crack in the earth that runs along the bottom of the Mississippi near New Madrid. This geological fault line does not worry them as much. Every day they must look out at this "Heaven" they've inherited or "the Land of Lincoln" that has come to them with the heft of history. These labels are taken seriously. Natives of the "Show Me" state, skeptical of even that skepticism they put on like a costume, occasionally will ask themselves an existential question. It must be hard to see through all the fable and legend, to picture who they really are. "Show me," they demand. "Show me."

The Flyway

In high school, I dated a woman whose father was an aerial photographer. He worked for the Fort Wayne newspapers taking ordinary pictures most of the time, but every once in a while he'd publish a picture taken from a plane. Often those photographs would be panoramas of the downtown or the extent of the frequent spring flooding. The most frightening shots were those of the occasional airplane crashes, the perspective from above dramatically capturing the path of the wreck as it cut into a woodlot, scarred a field, and ended in a heap of debris near a road. I always looked forward to talking with him about his photography and his flying. I arrived early to pick up his daughter. I chatted about basketball and the weather, all the time imagining him on his dangerous mission, leaning out of open doorways intent on his picture as the little plane he rode in banked and circled.

Huge blowups of his pictures were hung everywhere in town—in government offices and schools, as murals in restaurants and malls. In the hallways of the Memorial Coliseum, where I would take his daughter to watch basketball games, there were his pictures of the building itself being built, from groundbreaking to opening ceremonies. The banks and insurance companies used his pictures on their calendars and the local TV stations used them as props behind the fake windows on the sets of the local news. At Mike's Car Wash there was even a picture in the room where you waited while your clean car was toweled dry. I remember staring intently at these pictures whenever I came across them. I liked the effort it took to reorient myself to that elevated angle, how then I could better understand my relationship to the city I lived in. "You are here," I'd say to myself. And I knew where I was. I could see how it all fit together and how the city was whole and complete. From ground level, the world you walk through always seems more hidden. Rushing to turn a corner, you almost feel that you might catch someone finishing construction of the stage scenery you are walking through. The curtain wall of the street where you walk hems in the feeling for a place. It doesn't go very deep. But from above, there is depth. You can see the layers of walls and streets, trees and lawns, the fences and yards.

I wasn't the only one from my town looking at those pictures. We all did. Those pictures were maps cluttered with actual residue of our existence here. Our houses, not symbols of them, cast shadows. And we all saw ourselves connected to each other in this new way. These pictures did a real service. They helped us imagine us.

Those photographs also exposed something else to us. They made clear our exposure. It didn't matter what picture you looked at, those panoramas of my town always revealed the component of time itself as an ingredient of any place. I could always find in the pictures a building that was no longer there, a construction site that now had been topped off, a field that was now a road. The majestic sweep of the city, captured in flattering, elevated pose, at first looks so substantial and permanent, but on closer inspection confirms the constant flux of place.

This is not unusual to the Midwest. But to midwesterners it is perhaps more unsettling than to residents of other places in this dynamic country. Here, we tell ourselves, the static is a strength, picturing our landscape as a constant. We tend to think of this place almost as a reference we imagine the rest of the country uses to gauge their own ever-widening gyres away from the past and America itself. Here, we treasure the library of those sacred images: the farm with the red barn and windmill, the small town with its water tower like its own silver cloud hovering overhead, the county seat of domed courthouses and its fronting square, the cities planned and spacious, solidly built of limestone and paved with red brick. Here is *the* constant Main Street. Here is *the* Cafe. And yet the evidence of change is here also. In the photos on the calendars of insurance companies and in the jagged backlit skyline stills of the eyewitness news teams things change. Those photos we thought captured our substance also image our transitory existence. Like an X-ray image, these photos frozen in time reveal that all that seems solid can turn invisible when fixed on film.

There is no better example of this than the business of the aerial photographing of farms. Shoestring entrepreneurs fly over farmsteads and feedlots taking rolls of pictures and then try to sell a glossy print or two to the inhabitants below. I am sure my girlfriend's father must have shot a few rolls of farms on slow weekends. Every farm family I have ever visited had been approached by a photographer waving a contact sheet of shots of the farm even if they hadn't actually purchased a print. And those who did usually hung the image, framed, in the den above the desk or sometimes in the living room over the couch. The compositions of those pictures were always the same. The place was gorgeous and green. The mud always grown over with clover, the bright sunlight reflecting off the polished flanks of the gleaming combine. The farm below looked like *the* farm. The angle hid the slit trench garbage pit out behind the rusted wire corn crib. The eroding hillside was screened by the fountains of Lombardy poplars, their dusty leaves no doubt given a rich emerald patina by the use of a filter on the lens. The Platonic Farm floats in those frames above the davenports, levitates, suspended above countless mantelpieces. The cropped photo feeds our own desire to believe in this perfection and sometimes fools us into believing we have attained it. The image lodges in all of our minds. This, we believe, is how it has always been, how it is meant to be. Still, still we know, deep down, that things, no matter how hard we try, do not hold still.

There is another kind of exposure this aerial view conjures up. Namely, it shows us the fragility of our human works when nestled in the open fields. This point of view is the point of view of the tornado, the Midwest's own natural disaster. When I look down on these bucolic and bustling scenes, I see a recognizable neatness, meticulous attention being paid to the classical imperatives of balance and order. But I also see the space, chaotic and wild, that nibbles on the picture's edges. These farmsteads in their severe poses, the villages with their crisp grids of streets, seem sometimes as if they are merely stapled to a thin skin of the earth. The fields' checkerboard squares radiating away from the houses and barns seem about to burst at the seams of the section roads. The cities themselves don't sprawl as much as they advance crystalline, block by block, into the empty spaces that hems them in. They are surrounded by those deserts of corn and beans, and the fields themselves can turn back into grass and weeds at the drop of a hat if you don't take care.

A tornado, with its unbelievably delicate finger of wind, touches a spot of humid earth and unbuttons the uncontrolled physical forces midwestern energy and enterprise have worked diligently to hold in check. A storm is talked about not so much as the source of power itself but as some kind of magic catalyst that disrupts the adhesion of an ordered life. Thus, the stories of buildings ratcheted a quarter turn on their foundations or the livestock left dazed grazing in the trees. Houses implode, we tell ourselves, imagining the drop of pressure that animates the four solid and steady walls that have, until now, protected us. The tornado's route, the way it skips and meanders, is the antithesis to our own routes mapped into the land. The tornado wiggles its hips, a broken field runner on the limed gridiron. We try to channel it, gain control over it. We say there is an alley laid down through which the storms transverse the region, but it is our own wishful thinking. We don't really believe we can route these storms the way we drained the swamps, those ditches we now use to cower in while the tornado's fingernail tweaks our abandoned autos like tiddlywinks, sending them end over end down the road.

The photographer, focusing on the perfect scene below, twists the telephoto lens of his camera. So too does the tornado seem to target what's beneath. It is from the air that we usually see the aftermath of the destruction of the storm, the random pattern of debris, a fossil record of chaos. The click of the shutter and the camera fixes what it takes in. The tornado opens its eye and our walls begin to shudder. This kind of weather is the Midwest's worst nightmare. Tornadoes appear like those projected monsters in the fifties' science fiction movie *Forbidden Planet* generated from the buried images of the victims' ids. We couldn't ask for a better disaster, one more suited to the temperament and constitution of the midwesterner.

. . . .

A headline in the Des Moines *Sunday Register* also captured, for me, that midwestern character. The banner headline appeared in the newspaper's peach section, the special weekend sports supplement, during a particular stunning autumn when the University of Iowa Hawkeyes were undefeated through most of the football season. Alas, that Saturday, the day before, the team had been upset by a Big Ten rival. Sunday morning, we read about the game beneath these words: WINNING STREAK HAD TO END SOMETIME. I've since thought that fragment to be a kind of haiku that expresses the peculiar sensation of being midwestern, a homegrown variety of nice zen. Within its syntax is hidden the delicious mixture of pride and politeness, optimism and fatalism, a shy, aw-shucksing shrug that disguises deep disappointment. It is the perfect expression of the desire to make sour grapes into the sweet preserves you only serve to company. Midwesterners have this reputation for honesty, guilelessness, square shooting, but our utterances, baldly delivered, are often encoded with this subtle layering of paradox. Our speech is plain, it's true, lacking the urgency of the East, the innovation of the West, or the metaphor of the South, and yet it contains the grammar of the white spaces that spawn it.

It's not so much an expression of what's what as it is the tense of what is not.

Back in Fort Wayne when I was a kid, I would be reminded often by adults—parents, teachers, even strangers—that our town had been targeted during the Second World War by Hitler's Luftwaffe. This was my early lesson in the convoluted nature of the Midwest's mythology. What I noticed was that all of those storytellers—my mom and dad, my grandparents, the school crossing guard—delivered this message of doom with the utmost pride. The citizens of every city in the Midwest where I have ever lived have considered occasionally in the public print of their newspapers or the broadcasts of their talk radio stations that they, too, are on some ultimate list. There is, they mused, a bomb or a missile somewhere with our name on it even as the enemy changed and the weaponry evolved. Ironically, in those towns and cities, we slept easier at night knowing of our strategic importance to some master planner a world away. After a while, thoughts like these become second nature, another step in the dance we dance with ourselves as we cast about for evidence of our value. This is the roundabout way we brag on ourselves. We are envied for our unenviable positions.

The sky, then, sends us messages about ourselves. Sometimes, we look up and see our fellow Americans busily flying over, ignoring us. Sometimes, we scan the sky for weather that is a projection of our fears. Sometimes, strangely, we find ourselves looking for the telltale formation of bombers.

. . . .

Meanwhile, back on earth, we are busy constructing our own images that can be read only from above. Stan Herd, a farmer in Kansas, uses his tractor and plow and a palette of various grasses, grains, and legumes to etch in a field near an Indian school the portrait of Chief Saginaw. When asked, Herd likens his creations to the ancient native mound builders, whose massive earthworks still, after years of weathering, plot the likenesses of animal fetishes and mirror, in the orbit of the medicine wheel, the slowly rotating constellations overhead. The crescent moon redoubt the Hopewell people built in Indiana or the Grand Mound near Newark, Ohio, can best be read from the sky. We marvel while walking among the grassy hummocks and overgrown ditches of these sites. We are unable to put together in our minds the picture we are now walking in. Like walking through our cities, we find it hard to piece these bits of the landscape into a whole pattern. The Midwest is filled with these flattened Mount Rushmores. They are monumental all the same but just spread out. The people who built them could not fly. That fact leads the imaginative among us to posit a genesis of ancient landing fields for alien spacecraft. Perhaps their art was meant to create something that could not be seen or recorded, encoding the land with secret messages. We, with our airplanes, have stumbled onto something never intended to be seen. Who knows? What do we learn from these ancient messages? The farmer in Kansas, as he works, must imagine himself floating above his land canvas, a healthy exercise in sensing the scale of things. His vision is at once microscopic and vast.

When I moved to Iowa, I'd get myself invited to my students' farms. On weekends, I'd walk beans or stack hay bales. One fall, I found myself plowing a harvested bean field tucked between the Little Sioux River and the loess bluffs of western Iowa. I was driving a tractor that cost more than the house I had just bought. It had a heated cab and digital readouts of ground speed and exhaust stack temperature, RPMs and engine hours. I had tuned in the Sioux City public radio station where it was pledge week and, honestly, Vivaldi's *Four Seasons* played between pitches for money. The tractor steered hydraulically, humming as its hinged middle made the turns at the end of the field. It was easy to drive. Mr. Brown had showed me, before he turned me loose, the lever to lower the six-bottom plow and the throttle that moved between the international symbols of fast and slow, cartoon hare and tortoise. The field was huge, and there were no fences. I kept my eye on the distant horizon. I'd glance over my shoulder now and then. There the moldboard plow was turning over the rich black bottom dirt called gumbo. The sky was what my cloud chart calls chaotic, occluded, layered with blankets of thick clouds. It smelled like snow. I crept along listening to the donkeys braying in Vivaldi's Tuscan hills while all the time I was on a farm near Turin, Iowa. When I looked back again at my work, I was astonished to see hundreds of seabirds swooping down out of the gray sky and landing in my wake. Gulls and terns of several makes and markings, more kinds than I could identify, since I had grown up so far from any sea. I had been turning over a rich harvest of grubs and worms, and the birds on their migration along the ancient flyway of the Missouri River trailed me, circling and diving, as if I were a lobster boat setting pots. But at the time, it seemed miraculous. More birds arrived out of the lowering clouds, settled in the corduroy of furrows as if bobbing on waves. I had drifted along in my little routine, nestled inside the warm cab of a machine so sophisticated it runs itself, when the flocking of birds, newly arrived from the arctic, made clear my actions rippled outward from here, to places around the world and back and forth through time. I was just scratching away in a tiny corner of the earth sending messages I didn't understand to species I never knew existed.

Once again, I was caught up in the midwestern paradox. I felt, simultaneously, my isolation on one of the margins of the world and my connection to what is essential in the scheme of all things.

MANUFACTURING PLACE

My sense of place has been generated from a particular rust belt environment of manufacturing. I was aware, growing up in Fort Wayne, Indiana, that things were made there and that those made things contributed to the identity of the place. Trucks and all their parts, pistons and axles, electric motors of all kinds, rocker valves and gasoline pumps. Pumps, pumps of all kinds. Though my parents both worked in what we call now the service sector, I still have the peculiar disposition of taking the abstract and recasting it as a solid thing.

In Fort Wayne, as in many midwestern industrial cities, the factories were built on the east side of town. The prevailing winds are from the west, thus the location of a city's smokestack industry is downwind. Fort Wayne's east-end metropolis of factories and foundries informs a metaphor I find I use over and over: factories in the east manufacturing the lovely day and sending it streaming off the assembly lines out over my city. A union-made morning, a sunset built of scrap.

I heard constantly, as I grew up there, that Fort Wayne was

seventh on Hitler's bombing list. It is a folk legend of course and reflects what I recognize as a midwestern combination of pride and inferiority. Fort Wayne, it says, was important enough to be destroyed. As with many such legends, there is an element of truth in it. During World War II, Fort Wayne was strategic because almost all the magnetic copper wire was manufactured there. Today a significant percentage of wire is still made there, and the skilled craft of cutting the dies through which wire is drawn is still practiced there. I played on a Little League team sponsored by Indiana Wire and Die. Essex, Rea Magnet Wire, Phelps Dodge all sponsored such teams and were where my friends' parents worked. We all used cable spools for tables on our porches and patios. In Junior Achievement we made string-art sailboats using thread-gauge surplus wire. When the prevailing wind failed to prevail, you could taste the tang of metal in the air, it coated your tongue and plated the backs of your teeth.

In Fort Wayne, wire is everywhere.

. . . .

Last Sunday, as I have for the last twenty years since I left, I called home. My mother and father are fine, thank you very much. Even though, on either end of the line now, there is the synaptic leap of our voices through space—we use cordless phones—I still like to think, as we speak over the distance, of the actual wire. I think of the wire, the thread of insulated copper, that leads the signal singularly from my home now, in Syracuse, New York, to Home with a capital *H,* as simple as the analog transmission of voice via some vibrating string and two resonant tin cans.

I know. I know. I know about the microwave carriers, the towers studded with the arrays of lozenge antennae. And I know about digital switching, the scrambling of our words into binary pulses and their speedy translation back to an amplified, high-fidelity proximity of our original chit-chat. And I know about fiber-optic cable, data hitchhiking on a beam of bendable light. But I can still imagine that there still exists this physical umbilical to a physical place, an actual connection several hundred actual miles in length that conducts our conversation by means of the rhythmic jostling of charged metallic molecules, my weekly verbal wave, a boosted electric wave whipping through the medium of copper wire.

My father worked for forty years as a switchman for, first, the Home Telephone Company and, then, General Telephone Company once GTE acquired Home. Growing up, I would be taken along by my father while he troubleshot in the various switchrooms around the city. Those switchrooms were everywhere, but were hard to see. Many of them were housed in houses in residential neighborhoods to blend in with the houses that surrounded them. Often they were cinder-block shacks on back alleys or were mistaken for schools and office buildings. The main switches took up floors above the business offices of a central building downtown. These switchrooms were the mechanical replacements for the human operators who sat at boards and actually spliced, by hand, a call, lifting your one cable out of a tangled trunk line and then socketing home the connection on the panel before them.

The earlier automatic switchrooms my father took me to were noisy, a constant staccato of whirs and clicks as the switches prompted by the ratchet of a rotary dial somewhere counted out the number in rapid *tsks*, spinning, then suddenly taking hold with a crack, a kiss of bare wire leads, then the next number in a switch somewhere else in the room. The call hissed its way through the building. Hundreds of simultaneous calls being dialed mixed with the sudden release of the magnetic attraction, a *cajunk* of a hang up somewhere, when the circuit let go.

My father was in a switchroom when Kennedy was shot, knew something had happened because the switches went wild, the routine stutter and pop cranking up to an unrelieved storm of hailing. It was deafening, he said. He used an instrument called a Butt-In to butt in to a series of conversations, using alligator clips to tap the lines, and pieced together the unfolding story of the assassination.

Though noisy, the switchroom looked like the stacks of a library. The thousands of switches were dust covered with gray- or brown-painted thin metal shields shaped like the bindings of books. The switches were arranged in rows that ran the length of the room and in rank on floor to ceiling bookcase frames. Sliding off the shields—they had the heft of bound periodical volumes—was like taking a book from the shelf. There were even the same library ladders running on overhead tracks down the aisles with signs swinging from the eye-level step: Look Up Before Moving.

Often, too, a conversation would be playing on the scratchy speakers. I remember two people talking about the weather, shooting the breeze, making plans for the kids to come home. The switchmen were checking a line, had run the bad order through the PA system. The droning human voices mingled with the voice of the murmuring and twitching room, the sighs and the *tsks* of the switches reacting to or commenting upon the particular conversation's own inflections and tones.

During my own weekly ritual conversations home, the "I-am-fine-how-are-you" often seeming like an elementary lesson from a language lab tape, our dialogue's Q&A allows me time to imagine my voice, its rote response, as a plosive knot racing through the tunnel of cable, up and down over hills, buried and strung, the diffuse light as it crosses the estuary near Sandusky, the hairpin curve at Angola. Is it any wonder that I linger a bit in the switchroom as my electric signature finds its way through the nest of wire there?

For me, the switchroom with its transparent skeletal construction, its bare and functional schema, has always seemed to be a factory furiously manufacturing this idea of place, which exists in spite of the entropy of distance, against the tendencies of our drifting apart. The vented sound of the switchroom's workings, not unlike the trill of a sewing machine, stitched together these tenuous connections. When we speak of place we often speak of our sense of it, its constant though peripheral presence. That is, there is no such thing as a place, only our own inscription of it we carry around in our own nervous systems.

The switchroom, an actual place for me, is a cybernetic node at the same time. The switchroom, by facilitating these connections between people both local and long-distance, participates in the abstraction of place. The switches, tiny engines, churn out permutating transcriptions, address after address, of where *where* is. At the same time, the switchroom remains for me, by accident of my birth and my father's job, a "real" place, in my own wiring, though its function is to be transparent, a permeable membrane between here and there.

I see my father at his workbench, a broken switch disassembled before him, its voice now silent, its magic gone. I can hear the conversations too, the ones playing on the speakers, casual talk he's tapped into. This is where we are when we are in cyberspace, at this particular nexus, and the apparatus there, at least at one "there," was tended and maintained by my father.

The switchroom allows meeting at an imaginary spot that seems real, places like "Fort Wayne," say, or "Indiana," creating these places out of words, strings of words, spoken or, now, typed. And in the complete and convincing virtual construction of those shared places, we forget about these little offices, the actual precincts of our connections, these little libraries of wire.

. . . .

Wire. Connection to a place, for me, has never been difficult to grasp. That place, Fort Wayne, where wire is made and where my father spent his life parsing out pathways, that place is wired into my brain by means of its own self-produced tendrils, its gossamer of filaments and sparkling coils, a cybernetic neural net. For me to write about this place is to write about Place (with a capital *P*) itself.

Wherever I go, wherever I am, I see wire, wire that is going someplace, wire that has come from somewhere. I have seen wire strung in ancient Attic olive trees, on the floors of oceans. And as I write, I am wire—conductive, magnetic—because even though I am here, writing, I am also always, while writing, somewhere else.

WALKING BEANS

I know the exact moment when a future arrived in Iowa. I was on the Brown farm near Turin, in the western part of the state, getting ready to walk beans. I was standing on the edge of a soybean field, on bottomland near the Little Sioux River. The slopes and folds of the first line of loess hills still held a deep blue-green shade, the sun still rising behind them. Thayer Brown's pickup raced out of the hills toward us along the section of road to where I waited with his family.

My purpose in bringing up this moment is not to discuss the merits and the detriments of certain technologies. I said I was there when this one small part of the future arrived. I assume that other futures arrive daily. What interests me about this memory of this moment is how that moment was met. At that particular juncture the strategy was semantic, we were going to call a hoe a "hoe."

"Would you like to walk beans this weekend?" the Browns had said when they called earlier that week. I accepted the invitation on the strength of that turn of phrase, "walking beans," which had conjured up in my mind the visual pun of me leading legumes around by a leash, a notion I couldn't shake even when the Browns explained the actual procedure. And that procedure had sounded inviting as well, patrolling along the rows of beans with family and neighbors and then hoeing out the weeds we found there—cockleburs, sunflowers, burning bush, devil's shoestrings, and the volunteer corn sprouting from seeds spilled last year when the field had been planted to corn.

Thayer Brown had trucked out the new "hoes" we were to use that day. These "hoes" looked a little like the traditional hoe, a long handle attached perpendicularly to the business end of the implement. These "hoes" were not made of wood and metal, however, but were constructed from white plastic PVC pipe. A smaller tube had been joined to the larger gauge handle, and out of the ends of that smaller tube a length of nylon rope looped around. This was the wick, Mr. Brown told us. He was filling the hollow handles with a brand-new liquid herbicide. The chemical filled the handle and ran down to the wick of the "hoe" and saturated the rope. He capped off the open end of the handle and handed me my "hoe."

Walking beans this year would mean travelling the rows and painting the leaves of the weed with a lick of the wick, avoiding the beans since they were also susceptible to the chemical's workings. This was new. The herbicide was supposed to be absorbed into the vascular system of the touched plant, the poison drawn down into its very roots. In a week or so the weed would be dead.

The moment had happened, the future had been met. We proceeded to walk beans that summer in a manner farmers and their families, their neighbors, and hired town kids had been doing up until this moment, had walked beans. We talked as we walked and touched the weeds with our wands, the talk connecting me to past summers on the farm, in the way the bushy eruptions of volunteer corn harkened back to the particular arrangement of the farm the previous summer. With this new tool we continued to work.

. . . .

We know the world and the things in it by sorting the contents into distinguishable categories. Plants and animals, city and country, Iowans and non-Iowans. That day walking beans, we made the distinction between the leaves of the soybean plant and those of the weeds. But such categories are not always hard and fast. Last year's corn was a crop, but in this year's bean field, it's a weed. Boundaries between the groupings shift in response to the appearance of things new and, well, different. In response, we can expand our categories of perception or we can create new categories all together. Either strategy will work. Both approaches demand a significant act of imagination, a creative impulse, to entertain possibilities, to reorder the world in order to order it once again.

. . . .

Iowans used to say that, no matter where you were in the state, you were no more than ten miles from the nearest railroad. As that extensive system has contracted in this century, Iowans responded by converting many of the right-of-ways into one of the most extensive networks of bike trails and hiking paths in the country. This is an act of imagination, to envision corridors of recreation where once interurban railways and milk trains plied. To say this vision is imaginative is not, however, to say its leap was blind or wild. There is a practical logic at work in the creativity. Think about it. Using these abandoned stretches as public land keeps alive the connections between one another, and it is a hedge. Who knows when the economic winds will come again and when it might make sense once more to lay track? Iowans first saw a park could be made linear and then found a chance to bank some real estate for some future use.

. . . .

The writer Hamlin Garland called Iowa the Middle Border. On one level, we sense that somewhere within the borders of Iowa, the East ends and the West begins. But the Middle Border also implies that Iowa is the setting for many transformations, that here are biases for osmosis and change and, at the same time, paradoxically, the embraced notions of discrimination and order.

Look at the road map of the state and read it as the simultaneous expression of these two functions of borders. There is no other state in the union where the grid of roads and lanes so orderly traces the original boundaries of the township surveys. The pattern then expands exponentially into the rectangular sections that then crystallize into counties and then fall into tiers of counties. Iowa's patchwork pattern is the ultimate expression of being bounded, enclosed, defined.

And yet, at the same time, the very coordinates that demarcate one square mile from the next, the roads themselves, are, by their very nature, corridors of transmission. The roads aren't walls, after all, and though they separate and divvy up the land, they serve to communicate and connect. The end result is that the whole setup functions as a vast vascular system that saturates each bounded cell of soil with effortless access and egress.

. . . .

The experience of living here must be thrilling though subtle. Iowans at this moment are building another creative response to the shifting fortunes of the future. Those original townships, a highly imaginative invention of their time, always included a concession of land for schools. Consolidations of those original districts have forced Iowans to rethink the very idea of the classroom. The result is that the state has embraced a vision of a virtual schoolhouse, constructed out of satellite dishes, fiber-optic cable networks, and computers. Any corner of the state will be able to tap into expertise from any other corner of the state.

Iowans have seen the potential nature in all of these simple machines—fax, telephones, TVs, answering machines, CD players, PCs—as one big machine. Perhaps this is because, earlier, they were able to see that the individual functions of the mechanical reapers, binders, and threshers, which all derived from the original human practices of harvesting grain, could be combined into one machine, the combine. What Iowans are doing now is uncovering the essence of their appliances and applying them in brand-new ways.

. . . .

Iowa, the place itself, serves as a stage to confront the possibilities and choreograph the ramifications of human action and the passage of time. It seems to me that it is a kind of massive theater where these intense personal and communal dramas are played out in a setting that amplifies the very nature of the drama. It is no mistake that the *Field of Dreams* is the most telling of our cultural icons. W. P. Kinsella's original story incorporates in its main character this knack of seeing, when he imagines his farm as a baseball field. Perhaps even more telling is the actual existence of such a field. Created for the movie version of the book, the imagined set has taken on a life of its own. Near Dyersville is a monument to this habit of mind. A humble baseball diamond represents the space that is made for living and working amidst the dreaming.

. . . .

I have been trying to define here a kind of imaginative instinct to see the world in new ways by reordering the world as it is found. And I've suggested that it is the land itself which instructs Iowans on the nature of borders and shifting possibilities. I started this essay with a little pun which asked you to entertain for a moment an alternate way of looking at the phrase "walking beans." And for a moment you could imagine this upended vision of the beans themselves walking. Iowans seem daily to flex this metaphorical muscle. They get the jokes. They envision such puns. They chew the fat. They shake out the rug. These are creative and healthy activities. Such vision may allow Iowa and Iowans to escape the tyranny of the literal and confront the truly unexpected with a habit of mind that routinely questions habitual thought and practice.

. . . .

Consider for the moment those times in their history when some of their actual borders did get up and move. I am not talking metaphorically now. I am thinking of the most recent summer of floods when the bordering rivers and their tributaries quite literally left their beds and took a walk. It was a climatic rearrangement of the entire state. Remarkable, then, was the native response to the daily disasters. There was patience, persistence, good humor, and courage. The floods were surprising in their voraciousness and in their scale, but Iowans were not taken by surprise. Rivers had come to life amidst a population already expert in imagining the best and the worst.

. . . .

This last summer, I returned to the field near Turin. I wanted to show my six-year-old son the farm where, ten years before he was born, I walked beans. The Browns no longer walk beans. They drill them now, allowing the dense crop canopy to shade out the weeds. Mr. Brown sat my son on his shoulders and waded out, knee-deep, into the green sea of soybeans. The summer before, this same field was submerged beneath the green water of the Little Sioux River. I wanted my son to see this place and meet these people. I am hoping that a habit of thinking and acting will rub off. I hope that he can learn to see the metaphorical connections between an ocean and a farm field and come to realize this suppleness of thought is a special gift. Now, my son and Mr. Brown turn and call to me on this shore where I am looking out, trying to catch a glimpse of the breaking waves, the next future moment.

THE NIGHT SHIFT

After graduating with a degree in the writing of poetry from Indiana University, I returned home to Fort Wayne and discovered that my parents had sold my bed. It was a not-too-subtle hint that I was to make my way in the world. This is my family's style, to communicate by means of such gestures. We all knew, as my senior year came to a close, that I would commence with a liberal arts degree. We were just unable to make that fact mean anything. What is a poet supposed to do in Fort Wayne? The immediate answer was to force some action by rearranging furniture.

My old room was now occupied by my younger brother, and his room was now the TV room, where I was allowed to sleep on the couch until I landed on my feet. I stayed up late into the night. I outlasted the rest of my family watching television with me in my new room. Stacked against the wall were my boxes of books and papers. They were packed away in old cardboard meter crates my grandfather, who worked for City Light and Power, had liberated for me when I had left home. I have those boxes still, the sides printed with red and black graphics of residential meters, the spinning disks and numbered dials under a glistening snow-dome cover. In the flickering cathoded darkness, I imagined all those stored words coursing about on paper, pretended I could read the expended energy of my four-year effort. See, here was the measure of something, the hard wiring of a new nervous system, a capacitor of my future plans, a whole grid of knowledge I was lugging around with me. My father wouldn't get the conceit had I shared it with him. He'd fallen asleep on the floor, his head wedged up against the sofa's skirt. To him, they were boxes, dead weight, that he'd been hauling back and forth from Bloomington, up and down dorm stairs. He worked as a switchman for the phone company keeping another current of words flowing in a pipeline of jostling electrons, but he would never talk with me when I called home long distance from school. I woke him up when the screen turned to hissing snow.

In the weeks that followed, our silences became more elaborate with meaning. Something had to give. I started looking through the want ads and found a job for a night auditor at the Marriott Hotel. We lived then out near Northrup High School, and the hotel was right down Coldwater Road on the other side of I-69. I could walk to work, I thought. The more I thought, the more attractive it seemed. Getting off work at 7:00, I could climb into my brother's bed, still warm from his recent hibernation. I'd have a real place to sleep in the empty, quiet house during the day. And, working the graveyard shift at a hotel, I reasoned, would be a piece of cake. Check in a few straggler guests, straighten up the office, make a few wake-up calls—this would be my workload. I could even, my romantic mind spinning, in the time remaining, go about my real business, write a poem a night. The vision was becoming clear to me. The desk illuminated by the single lonely spot of light, me bent over the creamy paper scribbling, composing. The neon on the sign outside the door blinked off and on. What was that I heard? A solo sax's wail drifting in from the bar at closing time, punctuating my own deep sighs, etc. I skipped out of the house and headed for the hotel. I was qualified, I knew, for such an apprenticeship. I walked into the lobby of the hotel and asked to fill out an application for the night auditing job. In the blank that asked for the highest level of education I wrote that I had a BA in poetry.

Amazingly, that bit of information didn't stop Marty, the front desk manager, from hiring me. In my interview, after she allowed as the job would have some mathematics involved, I actually suggested that as a liberal arts major I had learned how to learn. I would start that night, I volunteered eagerly.

And that night, Dave and Pete, the other night auditors, introduced me to the NCR 442, a glorified mechanical cash register through which all the hotel's daily debit and credit had been registered. It was my job to balance the books each night and in so doing assure that the 264 room folios, or bills, were correct when checkout started early the next day. There *was* a little desk in the corner perfect for writing down that lyric in my head, but the desk had been set aside for me to run adding machine tapes of receipts of miscellaneous charges, phone calls, laundry, room service, bar bills. It took most of the night to post the charges and to run through the tub of room folios adding on that night's charge for occupancy and tax. I would do this with the NCR 442 in a special mode called "trail" so that each time I hit the total key the sum of all the charges got added into one big outstanding number. And sometime in the early morning, I was to push a special red button and the machine would spit out two numbers I was to compare. One was the summation of all the amounts due from all the customers recorded on their bills and the other was the summation of all the individual charges by category. You remember from grade school that adding the same group of numbers in any order will give you the same total, right? Those two numbers had to match exactly. And often in the early morning, after hours of entering figures into the machine and on to bills, I found the house, as we liked to say, was out of balance. Understand that this isn't a matter of throwing a few pennies in the drawer. Somewhere in all that paper was an adding or subtracting error. It was my job, I found out, to find it.

So I spent those long dark hours of the soul not writing poetry but trying to find a pick-up error where a clerk had punched in $44.56 instead of $44.65 when adding on new charges to a guest's bill. Pete and Dave were veteran auditors and had worked in dozens of motels and hotels. Pete told me that if we got robbed the thieves would probably shoot us since the lobby was a long way from the road, giving us time to call the police before the thieves got out of the lot. "They won't take the time to tie us up," he laughed. He audited the restaurant in the back by the switchboard. Dave stood out front, smoking while he ran room and tax. Dave showed me how to read the transaction tape as we scoured through the paper for a transposition error indicated by the telltale sign of divisibility by nine.

"Look," he said, "Pam is getting busy at checkout." Each clerk entered an identifying code. He reconstructed the day in the trail of blue numbers. Here, someone asking for change. Here, room 124 splitting off phone calls to be settled in cash and the room charge going to a credit card. Maybe the phone rang or kids ran through the lobby wet from the pool. Beth makes a posting error and then tries to correct it, adding when she should have subtracted, a businessman asking her for directions downtown. "Damn it, no!" Dave howled. "Nikkie should never touch this machine." The tape had unspooled into a huge Möbius clump at our feet. It was my job to roll it neatly, wind it back into a fist-size lump, and ship it as part of the package of receipts and reports we sent to the main office each morning.

If the night actually went smoothly and the paperwork was all out of the way by four, there still wasn't time to write. I would take fire walks through the hotel, check to see that the pilot lights were on on all of the water heaters. I'd check the teletype for reservations and replace the room keys in the appropriate cubbies. Soon it would be time for the wake-up calls, the crazy alarm clock with all the little levers set at fifteen-minute intervals. If someone who had left a message didn't answer the phone, we had to make sure he or she was up by going to the room. I'd take the master key ring attached to the hoop you could wear around your neck keeping your hands free. Usually, the guest was already up, in the shower or gone, the bill going on a credit card, but policy said we had to be sure. Pete would reminisce with Dave about the bodies they had found, people checking in to check out. Suicides always leave wake-up calls. "Remember to knock," he'd call after me.

In the quiet hallways, I'd think about how far this was from what I thought I would be doing. Waiting for the elevator I would try to compose something in my head. I was always groggy, an occupational hazard of working nights, a condition Pete and Dave assured me would wear off after three or four years. The keys jangled on my chest. I'd catch in the corner of my eye a ghostly me striding by the blackened windows in the hallway. True, I now had a place to sleep, but my brother's bedroom was never dark enough, the leaking daylight never quiet enough. Time now was much more concrete, and my body always felt stale. I had become too tired to sleep. Working nights does that. You begin keeping score of waking and sleeping hours as you try adjusting to life in both the day and night worlds. You pretend that the three restless hours you sleep right after work and the hour nap at mid-day and the couple of hours you doze in front of the television before eleven all add up to a sound eight hours. I was dreaming of numbers. I was day-dreaming at night. Always, as I entered a trance, I habitually hit the zero bar first to clear my brain of any hidden remainder, a top margin of nothings at the head of the tape. My hands as they rested anywhere searched for the calculator pads, my middle finger seeking out the little braille button oriented on the five. I didn't have to look anymore. The long columns of numbers, the time clocks, and the alarm clocks, the shifting modules of time, the beats to the line, and the rhythm, the rhyme of the body, everything was out of synch. "Wake up!" I'd call through the door after pounding. "This is your wake-up call!"

I'd been taught that when writing one entered a kind of dream state as well. But this was different. If I ever got a chance to write again I would be doing this writerly dreaming while actually walking around in a dream. This then, I understood, would be the way poems are really written, not just by me but by everyone, in between sleeping and waking, catch-as-catch-can, wading in the shallows of the everyday.

If I had had the energy to sit and concentrate, I probably would have dropped dead asleep. So I took to writing poems for hire again, a stunt some friends and I had tried in Bloomington. We would go up to people on the street and ask them if they would like a poem today. On any subject, we said. In any form. We'd write it on the spot in pencil on a legal pad or on a portable typewriter we'd tote along. Charge a quarter. We called ourselves RKO Radio Poems and our slogan was "A Poem Must Not Mean But Be 25¢." Now after work at the hotel, I caught a bus downtown to Friemann Square, a park tucked in between the City-County Building and the Fine Arts Center. The square had a reflecting pool, a statue of Anthony Wayne, shade and benches for the office workers who would wander into the sunken gardens and eat their lunches. I liked going up to people as they unwrapped a sandwich from the wax paper and volunteering to write a poem for them about anything they wished. On good days of fair weather the park was packed. I was another vendor drifting through the crowds. I was writing. I was writing something at least. I thought of myself as the sketch artist who talks with his model as he draws the pastel silhouette of his subject. I'd jot a line and try to coax a secret from mine. The sentiments of the love poems were Hallmark but I included the color of the beloved's eyes. I was clever enough and fast, building on a conceit built on cars if the subject liked cars or sports or flowers or even accounting. I knew numbers now. I spent most days that summer writing poems for strangers and pocketing quarters.

I found I was using old tricks to let me write while I thought. I used stock metaphors and epithets, like the rosy-fingered dawns Homer used, to cover myself as I thought up the next line. So many people asked me to write about the beautiful day, I just worked from the fact that midwestern cities like Fort Wayne always built their factories on the east side so that the smoke from the plants would be blown downwind by the prevailing westerlies. The day, then, was being manufactured there in the east, built on the assembly line of Zollner's and the Harvester, smelted in the wire works, wired in the GE plants and sent packing out over the city like the rosy-fingered dawn on the conveyor of blue sky. Etcetera.

> The graveyard shift's retooled the odds and dyed the evens
> so that tomorrow packs a list of options. Clouds rumble

off the assembly lines, belting out UL listed thunder. The stars have been recalled, surviving more or less the period of planned obsolescence guaranteed by the night before.

I learned a lot. The poems were prosey, clumsy, but I was face-to-face with an audience who brought to the exchange a whole passel of expectations and fears about the enterprise of art. I guess that was what I learned. To listen and to recover this kind of charged language, this Whitmanesque celebratory rhetoric, for people, and I was one of them, who had largely given it up having only confronted it while in school, which held the matter in a fiduciary limbo. I learned too that any subject can be made poetic, even Fort Wayne.

My mother and father watched me work the crowds. I'd see them screened by the patinaed flanks of Mad Anthony's horse. I must have been even more curious to them than to the indifferent citizens sunning in the square. They had sent me off to school on the float of savings bonds and second jobs, and I had come home to audit hotels and write pedestrian poems for a city that seems to live quite nicely, thank you, without the words. It was hard for my parents to tell if they had done their duty and propelled me into the next higher class. Where does a poet fit in? I took them to lunch on my quarters, at Coney Island on Main Street a few blocks down from the park. There, at the counter, I wrote a poem for them. I kept a copy.

At a Loss

The old glaciers sat here for centuries thawing and freezing. My parents met on a teeter totter at Bass playground across the street from Colone's store, beneath the Broadway GE sign that served as stars.

Every place generates its own mythology, the city's utilities.

Here we sit on the same fulcrum. We rise and fall reading the stars that never seem to burn out. Advertising that sells itself.

Garcia's Jesuit points down the Maumee as it flows back on its tributaries. General Electric reinvents heaven every night. A noun and verb find the proper playground, locating the creaking seesaw of our parents' actions.

I am here for now, but I am leaving taking the stories with me. About this place I am at a loss for anything more than words.

I'm not sure what my parents make of this, or what the inhabitants of a city like Fort Wayne make of its poets. In the presence of such worried words, more often than not, the response is a silence.

I began to write when I was a night auditor. To audit, I knew, was rooted in the Latin for hearing. Each night I gave the books of the hotel a hearing. In the moments between sleep and work, I had begun to write, but more importantly I had started listening to all those silences around me.

I am writing this essay in the middle of the night having let its deadline creep up on me. A few hours ago it became the day this bit of writing is due. This is to be finished today. This time of night, three in the morning, still feels the same, the weight of the silence and the keys under my fingers. I am still balancing a set of books. I have my own bed now and I lie in it. Finished, I can go to sleep.

CORRECTIONVILLE, IOWA

Pelisipia, Polypotania, Saratoga, Illinoia, Assenispia, Michigania, Cherronesus, Metropotania, Sylvania. Thomas Jefferson drew up a list of names for the new states northwest of the Ohio River. Since 1776, the Congress had been promising land to the soldiers who fought the War of Independence and had, at the same time, considered the sale of land in the new region as a way to raise money for that war. Now with the war over and the land being purchased from the tribes and ceded by the states with claims, Congress appointed two committees, one to plan for the governments of the new territory, the other charged with locating them and drawing up methods of their disposal. Thomas Jefferson sat on both committees.

I think of him sitting on top of his mountain in Virginia, not in the squat fireplug mansion of Monticello with its collections and contraptions, but in the little cubic cottage out back, the honeymoon house, the first building he put up after balding the hill. Through the mullioned windows he watched his slaves tend the latticework of gardens that stretched along the ridge, square beds divided into smaller squares. Before him he had a rough map of the territory under consideration. For his purposes, it didn't matter how accurate that map was. He had never been there, though George Washington had toured Ohio and even surveyed a few miles there. With a ruler, Jefferson drew a straight line north from the falls near what is today Louisville, Kentucky. The lakes, the rivers, the hills did not deflect the line. From his original meridian, he began to lay out squares of space that would eventually add up to new states that needed naming.

In Jefferson's list there is the goofy classicism. He screws the Latin endings onto the native names. Sitting in his little cottage, he is like a kid in a treehouse daydreaming about the secret club he is founding where everyone holds a title and everything is ordered and embedded in ritual. Of course Jefferson's musing isn't *like* the summer distractions of the neighborhood gangleader, it is exactly the same thing, the only difference being in the scale of the invention. It is not just a map of the backyards in the local cul-de-sac but a whole continent he is considering. I like very much the names he scribbled inside his neat squares. They contrast smartly with the severe and logical grid he generated to net up the beginnings of an empire. The names that did settle on those places are harmonics of those Jefferson toyed with. Michigan and Illinois echo the originals as if they are the final versions of copies of copies, only the main plosives picked out from the mumbling through time. But it is the chutzpah of the whole enterprise, the wicked inventiveness and brute reason that allowed him to sweep away the physical features of the west and cooly scale it down to human size.

There were compromises. Jefferson originally thought in hundreds, ten by ten mile squares. And his miles were the nautical kind, I don't know why. With the Ordinance of 1785, the

Congress of the Confederation created the office of the Geographer of the United States charged with surveying the new lands into six-mile by six-mile squares called townships. The land ordinances of 1784, 1785, and 1787 address how the recently independent colonies would handle their own colonial expansion and were platforms for confronting the issues of expanding slavery and extending human rights. Those laws prefigured the workings of the Constitution, being written in Philadelphia while the initial ranges were being surveyed in Ohio, and its first ten amendments. But I am more interested here in the physical residue of these acts, the scoring of the land with that waffle grid of true bearings.

. . . .

Recently, I came across a book by Joseph W. Ernst called *With Compass and Chain: Federal Land Surveyors in the Old Northwest, 1785–1816*, published by Arno Press in 1979. In it, Ernst explores how Jefferson's abstract ideas were made real. Ernst is consumed with procedure and the practical questions of implementing theory in the field. He records the surveyors' food and pay, their measuring instruments, their letters and notes, their payoffs and politics. These men walked every inch of the ground that would become the Midwest.

On September 30, 1785, Thomas Hutchins, the Geographer of the United States, sent his first survey notes to Congress:

> Based on observations made while running the E-W line from the North bank of the Ohio at point due north from Western termination of a line run as a southern boundary of Pennsylvania. 46 chains and 80 links West of this point, lands disposed for growth of vines. Variety of trees and bushes. The whole of the above described Land is too rich to produce Wheat, but is well adapted for Indian

Corn, Tobacco, Hemp, Flax, Oats, etc. and every species of Garden Vegetables, it abounds with great quantities of Pea Vine, Grass, and nutrias weeds of which cattle are very fond and on which they soon grow fat.

33 Chains, 14 links, which make a mile from the Meridian, High land.

22 Chains, 37 links, the land is extrodinary good, and in some places it is too rich for Wheat, where fine Meadow may be made. Timber Locust, Black Walnut, Mulberry, Hickory, Elm.

21 Chains, crosses a ridge, land between good, in several places it is tolerably free from brush or underwood.

6 Chains, 60 links, brook running South 20 degrees West.

14 Chains, 40 links, steep narrow ridge nearly 170 feet high, perpendicular. Covered on east side with many bushes and weeds. Golden rod, the latter when timely used and properly applied has been found efficacious in curing the bite of the most venomous Snake. Soil on the ridge equal parts sand and black mould.

13 Chains, gradual descent, thicket with trees, the whole of this distance was cut through for the Chain carriers to pass.

5 Chains, 63 links, makes two miles.

In the first two miles of his survey, Hutchins plows through a sheer ridge face, fords a stream, and clears a straight blaze through a thicket. As the geometry of his task draws him straight on, his eye is drawn to this new, new world in his periphery. He sometimes reports what he finds, but of course he sees deeper into what he sees to what can be used and exploited. He is musing on the proper order of domesticating the wilderness. It is another act of imagination. In his mind, he imports the grain and crops. A pedestrian Adam, he names the trees he finds while at the same time he pictures the lumbering. It goes without saying the timber's sectioning, milling, and planing follow. Its metamorphosis into furniture and into the wagons to haul it to new houses is the final destination. He brings the garden to the Garden. His vision even includes the metabolism of the native weeds into the fat on cattle. He gets carried away here, a touching flourish, empathizing with the livestock. He almost breaks into narrative. This flight of fancy is made even more tender when the reader remembers that its writer is mired down in mire, swamp and jungle, bitten by bugs and ever conscious of those venomous snakes. Linking it together is the stretching of the chain itself, inching along the ground, another snake, rattling over rocks and hollow logs and fresh-cut stumps, sizzling through the grass as it is reeled back in. Sound has come to the forest, the haunting racket of the ghosts to come trailing the forged, precise shackles of their vices. There is someone here now who will hear the trees falling.

In the geographer's notes as well, there is another story. While he suggests the cultivation of Indian corn and tobacco, his eye is peeled for the Indian himself. His survey had already been delayed by skirmishes, his stakes and corner markers would be destroyed once he moved on. The American incursion into the lands northwest of the Ohio River would proceed in its crystalline manner, square by square, but it was preceded itself by the most irregular pattern of purchase, conquest, or acquisition. In contrast to the logic woven by the patient web of townships, a midwestern map of treaty cessations looks like the splotches of woodland camouflage. The patches of Indian territory sold or won were being chewed away from the edges by opportunists and speculators. The water routes took the Europeans far inland where they struck out from the forts at Detroit, Chicago, Louisville, and St. Louis. The irregular shapes of the treaty lands, their borders fixed not by compass and chain but by the land itself, rivers, lakes, and hills, suggests the anarchy of their taking, a swipe here, a swath there.

Which is more terrifying? This random rent or the steady quilting? Perhaps they were worse taken together, the chaos so reasonably ordered and camouflaged by the brand of that order which remains cut into the land today.

. . . .

No other feature so marks the midwestern landscape as the signature of townships. The six-mile squares broke down into thirty-six sections of one square mile each, and each square mile of 640 acres reduced to those plots of recognizable dimension, the eighty, the back forty. There is nothing natural about it. It is not like the Spanish moss drooping from southern trees or the dripping ferns of the Pacific Northwest, nor is it like the rocky scrabble in the soil of the East or the dusty reaches of buttes and mesas in the West. We know the Midwest by this arbitrary and artificial pattern that has been imposed upon it.

Though most of the public lands outside of the original colonies and the South were surveyed into these grids, it is this chunk of land stretching from Ohio west to Minnesota and Iowa where its pattern is most deeply inscribed. Here the subtlety and variety of the region's topography and ecology cannot suppress the imposition of the grid. Further west, the landscape becomes much more spectacular, space an identifying feature in itself. The people are fewer, and they begin to speak of the land in sections, not acres. Historically, the Homestead Act of 1862 changed the focus of land claims. Individual settlement powered land acquisition west of the Missouri River, not the communal motives that informed the original ordinances. The grid "took" in those more eastern states, and, though the townships' governing structure has withered away in many places, it hasn't in all places by any means. What survives is the network of roads and fields, oriented north to south and east to west and measured out on a human scale of rods and acres that scores this place.

The Midwest, then, began as a highly abstract work of the imagination and lingers so today. The power of the grid that overlays it often prevents us from seeing the place itself. It has been characterized from its inception in two dimensions alone, flattened by fiat. At the same time, for those of us from the Midwest, this plane geometry that enmeshes us might be the only connection we have between us. What links the autoworker in Detroit with the actuary in Des Moines, the mussel digger near Galena with the strip miner near Athens? Perhaps it is only this thin tissue of coordinates plotted a long time ago that can tie together this region's inhabitants. We are midwesterners because we think ourselves into the map of the place without having to fit into the place itself. We relate to each other on that mathematical plane alone.

. . . .

I didn't know it then but the borders of my own neighborhood where I grew up in Fort Wayne, Indiana, were streets that followed the original township grid. My mother had set State Street on the north and Tyler Street on the west as the limits of my range. There was one exception. I could be ushered across those busy streets by watchful safety patrols to Price Elementary School, sited at their intersection. On the south was Spring Street where we lived. On the eastern edge was the smaller square of Hamilton Park.

But within this one-square-mile border, developers had carved out streets with asymmetrical abandon. A map of those streets looks like a cross-section of the burrowings of a colony of termites. Jefferson thought the grid to be the most democratic of forms. North Highlands, my neighborhood, the first suburb in town, was having nothing to do with democracy. Its larger houses, brick with drooping awnings, were perched on hills, at the prows of parabolas. There were pockets of cheap ranch houses set off behind massive clapboard four-squares positioned off-center on oblong lots. The roads followed the contours of the land. The land had been bulldozed, before the subdivision, into the traps and bunkers, the roughs and fairways of a golf course. A friend of mine lived in what had been the club house. Its lawn still had patches of the practice green disrupting the blue grass like a strange weed infestation. It seemed you were meant to get lost in the winding streets as if they were a defense against invading hordes from the greater city who could then be defeated in the maze of tree-lined streets. The neighborhood was a watered-down version of vernacular villages of Greek Islands where the whitewashed buildings tumble down a hillside. Its warren of alleys and double-backs were defensive measures against pirates. Here, the houses were all detached, the only raiders the armies of children free to run wild in the yards between them.

Before the golf course, the land had been owned by the Hamilton family. Some of the street names were Edith, Alice, Ida, Jesse, names of the Hamilton children. Edith grew up to be the great popularizer of ancient Greek myths. We read her book, *Mythology*, in our language arts classes at school. Growing up in Fort Wayne, I read about Perseus and Medusa, and Theseus in the labyrinth.

Hamilton Park had those steep hills because it had been, before it was grassed over, a trash dump. I played in a ruin. The grass covered the terraced steps of the sides where dogwoods, redbuds, and flowering crab apples had been planted. Rows of lilacs outlined the square rim of its top lip. There were ball diamonds, tennis and basketball courts, and picnic tables where you could play Rook at the bottom of the pit. When it rained water collected on the floor of the sunken park, and, sometimes, bits of the buried trash would work its way back to the surface. All of the kids had collections of their finds, shards of blue glass and Bakelite buttons.

I look back now and see how this little patch of ground surrendered up its history, how too it was a frame for the larger histories of the world. I realized that the stories of this place were just beginning to be told. Platting the landscape, subdividing the subdivisions of property would not be enough to kick start a culture of storytelling. We who grew up in the Midwest would have to sit here a while, within the borders of our own defined neighborhoods, on the banks of a natural theater, and watch as the junk of our too recent past resurrected itself and appeared to us as treasure in the dust at our feet.

. . . .

In Iowa, the idea of the township was raised to the nth degree. The squares of the sections quilt the larger squares of the townships that form the squares of the counties. It is a joke in Iowa that there is only one diagonal road. From the air, Iowa looks like a rumpled crossword puzzle. The squares spell out the season in an alphabet of three green letters—corn, beans, pasture—that alternate with the ink-black turned fields. Driving through the country on all those straight roads, I could check my odometer with the regular rotation of features. Intersecting road, corn field, soybean field, lane, corn, bean, house, bean, corn, road. A midwestern mantra of quarter-mile heartbeats. In Iowa, as you drive, you can string together a rosary of small towns as well that punctuate the rhythm of the spaces between.

Cottonville leads to Garry Owen, Garry Owen to Cascade, Cascade to Monticello. The towns are like knots in the chains the surveyors used. The towns can go together to form a kind of picaresque story line. Driving through Iowa can become a kind of modern walkabout, the water towers painted with the pictographs of town names, booster slogans, and zip codes rise up to meet you like giants on the horizon.

Once, I strung together a story that drew me west. Starting from Spillville in the northeast corner of the state, I vectored to Hospers in the northwest. In between was the town of West Bend. It takes three points to draw a line, and the line I sketched followed US 18 as it stepped north or south occasionally shooting across the state. The towns were linked by an eccentric geometry. Each contained the life's work of bachelor folk artists. In Spillville, brothers had built gigantic wooden sculptures housing clocks. In West Bend, a priest had constructed a grotto dedicated to the Virgin on the lawn of the church. In Hospers, a citizen sculpted a garden of painted concrete statues for the town square. Each of these creations is amazing in itself, but I find the parallels of their creation more interesting.

You learn that the artists never traveled more than a few miles from their homes. The wood for the clocks, you hear, was shipped in. Butternut, grapefruit, mahogany, teak arrived by trains whose conductors on their travels were always on the lookout for the fresh scrap of lumber, a new bark to peel. The shells and semiprecious stones that encrust the bubbling chambers of the grotto were also imported. Quartz and coal, fossils and pumice. The corals of the tropics grew on the thickening reef in West Bend. The artist in Hospers took his models from the books he read. Sculptures of Carrara marble were copied in the medium of cement. The worldly contributions to the art came into the hands of resolutely local artists, and yet each of them included in their elaborate schemes a piece or niche or grouping dedicated to the act of travel itself. There is a history of transportation clock, a tower of Babel wedding cake with marching bas-reliefs of vehicles topped by the legend "Time Flies." There is also a clock commemorating Lindbergh, a globe carved up with latitudes and longitudes cutting through the swirling clouds of the wood's grain. The grotto blesses mobility. Do I remember a side altar of the flight into Egypt? In Hospers, another history of transportation includes a green tractor in the evolution from dinosaur to rocket ship. The tractor is rendered most realistically. Its models burbled through the town as I toured. The artist swiped the paint for his tractor, the green Deere shade, from the local machine shop.

The clocks must stay in Spillville. They were willed to the town on that condition. The grotto is rooted to its lawn in West Bend. The garden of melting statues is cemented to its square in Hospers. I like how all of these artists recognized their own boundaries and then constructed a few more but still managed to elaborate, to the extreme, their chosen art. Once they defined their labor to such narrow tolerances they seemed to have found an infinite source of freedom. The clocks, the grotto, the sculptures are amazing, literal mazes of their creators' visions. They play all the variations within those limits.

Think of the Midwest as a vast plane studded with nodes of creation where artists are making a place by staying in place, riddling it with possibilities. Some, like the artists of Spillville, West Bend, and Hospers remain physically in the places they are creating, while others take their places with them. Those who travel still worry the fragments they take with them from their given coordinates, pieces of the true cross.

. . . .

You can draw another line through Iowa from Dubuque to Sioux City. That line would be the western extension of the northern border of Illinois. It also forms the northern border of a tier of counties in central Iowa. Remember that counties in Iowa are laid out in a regular pattern of squares that replicates the township squares forming those counties. Just south of the Dubuque line there is a parallel line called a correction line. The county boundaries running north and south take a little jog to the west along this line so that this tier of counties isn't exactly square but whittled down a bit as they head north. The correction allows a two-dimensional surveying system to be placed on the spherical globe. Reading *With Compass and Chain,* I learned that not only did the surveyors of the townships have to struggle with the physical burdens of their task but they also had to face the geometric paradox of their assignment. They were charged with squaring the earth. A correction line was one of their solutions.

Correctionville, Iowa, sits in the notch of correction between Ida and Woodberry counties. When I lived in Iowa, I always wanted to visit the place where theory butted up against reality. I never made the trip, but in my idle moments, I did like to speculate what the small town might be like. I imagined a Main Street filled with shops making minor adjustments to small engines, bicycle seats, and television sets. A town of photo retouchers, glass blowers, paint mixers, piano tuners, tree pruners, barbers, and tailors. Every house would need fixing up. In my mind, Correctionville was a kind of rheostat regulating the flow of all the forces coursing through the Midwest. The Delphi of tinkering. The epicenter of alteration. The mecca of dentists.

"We don't have the prison, that's for sure!" Maude Schemmel told me. "People usually think we have the prison here."

I had called the town clerk in Correctionville thinking I could have a city map sent to me. I thought I could find out if there was a chamber of commerce and when the library was open. I called the clerk, but Maude Schemmel, the librarian, answered the phone.

"I answer the phone when the clerk is out of the office," she told me. "She answers the library phone when I'm not here." A cybernetic logic behind this, I thought.

I told her that I knew the town wasn't the seat of the penitentiary and that I called because I was interested in the correction line, in townships, and in mapping. We talked about the town name and its history. She would send me their bicentennial booklet. Then we got lost while talking about geography and charts. I told her about the Greenland problem, how the island isn't as big as it looks like it is on certain maps.

"It depends upon the projection you use. Every map distorts the world some way," I said. "Iowa uses a different projection than Illinois or Indiana. They want their maps to be more accurate running north to south."

I continued, not really knowing what I was saying. For a moment I became confused and suggested that the correction corrected something on the earth itself instead of on the map of it.

Maude said, "You mean if I started walking due north from Correctionville, the miles would get longer the farther I went?"

"Only if you were walking on a map," I said vaguely. I was distracted by the picture in my mind of the librarian striding across the map of Iowa, crushing the names and numbers, trampling the ideograms of campsites and rest stops. I also thought about Thomas Hutchins, the first Geographer of the United States, as he stepped off into Ohio dragging his chains behind him, the ones he would use to try to shackle the planet.

I had exhausted the limited expertise I had in the matters of cartography when Maude asked her final question.

"But what if the map was as big as the world?"

. . . .

I'd like to go to the real Correctionville someday. I have been living and working as a writer in the other Correctionville, the one in my mind. There, I am constantly tinkering with the maps of the Midwest, trying to damp the distortions as much as possible while realizing that each selected vision of the place is a map more detailed than the thing it represents.

The Midwest is unique for this framework of squares stretched across the landscape, this cage of reason that has never quite fit. It is ground that has been imprinted, literally. It comes to us with its own fractal geometry where the smallest of its parts replicates itself on ever larger scales. All the efforts of politicians and surveyors to net up the region in knowing has not begun to capture the spaces between the weave. To write about the Midwest is to cast a web in those spaces and then wait patiently for things to begin to stick.